CONTENTS

Dedication   4
Glossary   5
A Word of Appreciation   6
Foreword   8
Preface   12
Introduction   17
1. Searching for My Family's Killers   40
2. Marched to a Grave   57
3. Living with Anger and Denial   77
4. The Shadow of Darkness   92
5. Forgiveness   107
6. Reconciliation   126
7. Blessings   170

Contact the Author   192

DEDICATION

This book is affectionately dedicated to the memory of:

1. My father, Soeum Himm
2. My mother, Kimcheav Ry
3. My oldest brother, Sophoan Himm
4. My older brother, Pinith Himm
5. My older brother, Piney Himm
6. My older sister, Sopheavy Himm
7. My younger brother, Sokmeth Himm
8. My younger brother, Sopheak Himm
9. My youngest sister, Somaly Himm
10. My younger brother, Sophat Himm
11. My youngest brother, Thlok Phirun Himm
12. My sister-in-law, Sophanny Sar
13. My nephew, Sophoan Himm Junior

All these close relatives were killed in 1977 under the Khmer Rouge regime. Then on 18 March 2004 my dear brother-in-law Chhunly Hourt was shot dead by two robbers who stole his motor bike.

GLOSSARY

angkar	=	organization
angkar loeu	=	higher organization
bong	=	older brother or sister
chao	=	grandson or granddaughter
chlop	=	Khmer Rouge secret agent or investigator
Khmer Rouge	=	Khmer Communist or Red Khmer
khmang	=	enemy
mak	=	mother
mith	=	comrade
'new liberated people'	=	those who lived in the cities or outside the Khmer Rouge's zones before the country was liberated on 17 April 1975; also called '17th of April's people'
'old liberated people'	=	those who lived in the Khmer Rouge's zones before the country was liberated on 17 April 1975
pa or *papa*	=	father
pook	=	father
ta or *tata*	=	elder, elderly (male)
'sent to school' or 'sent to study'	=	to be executed

A WORD OF APPRECIATION

First of all, I thank God, the Father, Son and Holy Spirit, for sparing my life during the darkest period of the entire history of Cambodia when the Khmer Rouge ruled the country. He has brought me back to my homeland even though I vowed never to return, in order to meet my family's killers and forgive them. Without God's richest grace in my life, this would have been impossible.

I thank my dear wife, Sophaly Eng, my beloved son, Philos Reaksa Himm, and my beloved daughter, Sophia Reaksa Himm, who have brought me great joy in life. They have given me the freedom to sit down in front of my computer and write this book. I wish to pay tribute to my only surviving sister, Sopheap Himm, who has grieved with me for years and who encouraged me to be careful when making my trip to meet our family's killers.

I thank my prayer supporters Cerintha Chia, Rebecca Lee, Emily Quek, Ramsay Chan, Dr Brian Stiller, Ron Apperley, Margaret Gilligan, Ammee Chung, Layswan Goh, Stephen Fong, Alvin Dahl, Ron Terry, Neel and Pam Reynolds, Randy Kimlin, Dr William Craig, Dr William Wan, Lee Wong, David Wong, Dr Nancy Craig, Dr Duc Nguyen, Dr Coung Nguyen, Kavin Nguyen, Mark and Doris Duesling, Ruth and Wayne Duesling, Rudy and Sharon Dirks, Henry and Tina Dirks, Art and Helen Andres, Dr Mark Sandercock, Sandi Sandercock, Dr Alan Kirk, Bob

Kirk, Larry and Mona McGill, Scott and Cynthia Veals, Chuck Ferguson, Pastor Timothy Phua, Dr Gus Konkel, Dr Jon Bonk, Elizabeth Davey, Lionel Sloggett, Hwee Ping, Chiang Hai, Dan and Rose Blosser, David Robinson, Ivor Greer, Este MacGregor, Evelyn Armstrong, Solina Chy, Jim and Agnes Verners, Johanna Webster, Revd John Wallis, Kok Liang Tan, Carolyn Ulrich, Phil Ulrich, Simon Koh, Dr Sorpong Peou, Richard Botkin, Thomas Chau and James Bo, Seap Loeuy. I really appreciate their consistent prayer for my ministry in Cambodia. Without their prayer support, I would not be able to serve the Lord there.

I also thank Pastors Narath Pann, Vansan Hong and Sokcheat Chea, who helped me to travel to the village where my family was killed and meet their killers to forgive them.

I thank many people in Northern Ireland who have encouraged me to write this book on forgiveness, based on my own experiences. My thanks especially go to Ian and Carol Little and Alan Little, Pastor Victor Maxwell, Trevor Watson and Ronnie Dawson and my friends Ken Rogers, Gwen and Roy, who helped me to share this message of forgiveness in many churches.

In addition, I thank my church-planting partner Pastor Pak Soon Lau, who willingly suffered with me after my brother-in-law was killed by robbers who stole his motor bike. Without his emotional support and encouragement, I would not have been able to stand firm in my ministry or even write this book. Finally, I would like to thank Pat Gerbrandt, who spent a lot of time polishing this book and Brenda Sloggett who helped with its final preparation..

FOREWORD

It was a great privilege for me to have been Sokreaksa's professor when he was a student at the Tyndale University College. We lost touch with each other for many years, and when he finally tracked me down in Singapore, he told me that he had been searching for me relentlessly. That is exactly the person he is. If I may use one word to characterize Sokreaksa, the word 'perseverance' comes to mind. He simply does not give up!

Anyone reading his book *Tears of My Soul* will agree with me that Sokreaksa persevered against all odds when he

- found himself alive among the dead;
- decided to find refuge outside Cambodia;
- landed in Canada as a refugee;
- enrolled as a student in college and seminary;
- succeeded in establishing his own small business in Canada;
- dedicated himself to return to his birthplace as a church-planter.

Most of all, Sokreaksa persevered in getting to the root of his existential problems – he was imprisoned by bitterness, hatred and a desire for revenge – and he persevered in allowing God to release him from that psychological prison by forgiving those who had inflicted such profound pain in his life. He persevered in understanding the need to forgive, the desire to forgive and the actual act of forgiving his enemies face to face. More significantly, Sokreaksa genuinely attributes this perseverance to live, to learn and to forgive to the grace of the Almighty God, the Father of our Lord Jesus Christ.

This is a true story that must be read and digested by everyone who harbours any bitterness or anger or an unforgiving spirit. As Sokreaksa himself discovered, the lack of forgiveness is often excused by one's sense of justice. Steve Asterburn labelled it 'justifiable resentment'. When evil is so unmitigated, it would appear so unjust to forgive, especially those who are not even repenting of the evil they have committed. The injustice done to Sokreaksa and his family is truly unmitigated, and yet he forgave in the way God has forgiven us. In contrast, the injustices done to many of us who have suffered betrayal and ingratitude in the micro-politics in our churches – politics played by small-minded, ambitious and highly insecure people – pale into insignificance when compared to the magnitude of the injustices done to Sokreaksa and his family.

In the comfort zone of our cosy churches we sing with gusto songs such as:

God hath not promised skies always blue,
Flower-strewn pathways all our lives through.
God hath not promised sun without rain,
Joy without sorrow, peace without pain.

But God hath promised strength for the day,
Rest for the labour, light for the way;

Grace for the trials, help from above,
Unfailing kindness, undying love.

God hath not promised we shall not know
Toil and temptation, trouble and woe.
He hath not told us we shall not bear
Many a burden, many a care.

God hath not promised smooth roads and wide,
Swift, easy travel, needing no guide;
Never a mountain, rocky and steep,
Never a river turbid and deep.

Words: Annie J Flint, 1919

But a little trouble, a little misunderstanding, a little unhappiness caused by others, and we become bitter and resentful. Reading this book should give one a right perspective to what a godly man means when he sings about 'toil and temptation, trouble and woe'. What Sokreaksa has experienced and committed to writing should also help us to realize that 'loving our enemies' is never easy. To love our enemies implies that we must forgive them first. Forgiveness liberates us to love. That unforgiveness imprisons our spirit is now a psychiatric fact. Unforgiveness is detrimental to our physical, mental, emotional and spiritual wellness. This phenomenon is now widely studied by the professionals in mental health. Ten years ago there were only 58 published studies on forgiveness. Today, there are more than 1,200.

When Sokreaksa, by faith, chose to forgive, he found himself freed from the shackles of nightmares and fear. He found himself stepping out of existential darkness into the marvellous light of possibilities and potentials. He found the truth that forgiveness is not so much about liberating the forgiven, but that the forgiving person liberates himself. It is in this self-liberation that Sokreaksa finds healing for his pain.

By his life and ministry the author has also communicated very important lessons on the pilgrim journey of faith. We often think that forgiveness is given only to those who deserve it. Those who deserve it are those who apologize and seek forgiveness. Nothing can be further from the truth. If we truly understand what the Lord Jesus has done for us, we will realize that none of us deserve God's forgiveness. It is something given to us when we least deserve it. There is no way that the Khmer Rouge lackeys who committed such heinous crimes deserve Sokreaksa's forgiveness. But he gave it anyway – it is his gift of grace in the name of Christ to those who killed his family.

I started out thinking that I was writing this Foreword as a teacher of Sokreaksa. But at the end of this brief journey, I am penning this as an unworthy student of one who had suffered much 'toil and temptation, trouble and woe', and yet forgave. My own 'toil and temptation, trouble and woe' are rather small and insignificant when compared with Sokreaksa's, and I have yet to learn how to forgive. My personal struggles as a lawyer concerned for justice and a Christian desiring to be forgiving are even more intensified after reading this book. There is still much for me to learn from Sokreaksa about forgiveness. Perhaps, by God's grace, I will be where he is in due course.

Revd Dr William Wan
Formerly Vice President and Dean, Ontario Bible College
(now Tyndale University College). Presently a Partner in the
Kelvin Chia Partnership, Singapore. February 2006.

PREFACE

Early in 2005, my former professor, Dr Jonathan J. Bonk, invited me to speak to a leadership conference at the Overseas Ministries Study Center (OMSC) in New Haven, Connecticut. I spoke to audiences about my personal experience of forgiveness. Prior to this conference, my professor had asked me to write a short paper of my story and submit it to him so that he could pass it on to the participants to read before they attended the conference. After reading it, the participants wrote short questions so that I could interact with them. I received more than fifty significant questions from them. I could have written another book based on these questions, but there were two relevant questions about the general experience of forgiveness in Cambodian culture that have captured my attention:

> 1. Your story and paper is very moving. Thank you for sharing it. Please tell us, are there others in similar situations who have been able to forgive those who killed their family and relatives and been able to repay such evil with kindness? Please talk about the spiritual resources for such forgiveness and the results that flow from it.

I returned to Cambodia six years ago and have observed that few Cambodians who suffered during the Khmer

Rouge regime have ever discussed forgiveness. Our culture teaches us to suppress our feelings as a part of self-
defence. Most are unable to deal with the deep pain they
have suffered from past traumas because they have tried
to bury these memories for years. Talking about forgiveness and disclosing painful emotional problems to out-
siders brings intense shame and disgrace in our culture.
Cambodians believe they must wear a mask to hide their
problems and carry them alone. We are taught never to
lose face or experience shame and humiliation in either
our private or social lives.

Another factor is that the concept of forgiveness in
our society is understood as enabling us to bury the past,
start a new life and never wake up those ghosts again. I
do not believe it is possible for Cambodians to start a
new life without dealing with the brokenness and
wounds in their lives. I spoke to a Buddhist monk in
Phnom Penh about my experience of being forgiven by
Christ, and how I had to overcome painful memories,
hatred, anger and bitterness. I told him of my visit to see
my family's killers and forgive them. He listened to me
patiently, but replied, 'The way you speak about forgiveness is not good for you. I can see that you endured torture twice – once the Khmer Rouge soldiers hurt you and
now you hurt yourself again. You need to bury your past
in the grave, and don't resurrect it or you will continue
to suffer. I lost my parents too, but I learned to deal with
it by burying the painful feelings; once buried they stay
in the grave forever.'

I felt he expected me to praise him for overcoming his
pain by burying it, and I did not know what to say to
him. He had his own philosophy for handling his sorrow.
I travelled that way myself, but it did not work, and my

concern is this: how can he live with unresolved grief? Or is it possible for him to forgive by burying his past?

It is very rare for Cambodians who lost their families or relatives during the Khmer Rouge regime to return, meet the killers and repay this evil with kindness. For men, revenge is interpreted as a sign of honour, and failing to carry this out brings disgrace to the family. In general it is difficult for Cambodians to forgive and almost impossible for them to bless those who have harmed them. I believe God's purpose in sparing my life was that I should take this message of Christ's forgiveness to the broken people of my country. He has given me strength to overcome an evil intention and turn it into a blessing. Only his abundant grace could so energise me to accomplish this difficult task.

> 2. What is the place of reconciliation and confession in forgiveness when there are heart-wrenching tragedies such as the one you have described? Have those who committed the atrocities in Cambodia confessed their wrongdoing and then been reconciled to those they tortured and humiliated, or is forgiveness a precursor to reconciliation which then brings about confession?

In this broken, tragic country there is no provision for reconciliation because no one understands it, but sadly, there is a monument to the Killing Fields. Before Pol Pot died, he refused to admit that he had taken the country into hell or that he had led it into the Killing Fields. He maintained that he was not responsible for the deaths of almost three million innocent Cambodians. Pol Pot's death in the jungle along the Thai–Cambodian border in 1998 captured the attention of the world. I was invited to speak on National Television in Canada, and was asked how I felt about his death. I responded that I was disappointed that Pol Pot died before making a confession of the evils he had done to his countrymen. I wished I could hear that he had asked for forgiveness from the Killing Fields survivors, as that would have helped, at least to some extent, to ease the pain of many people.

About three years ago, Khieu Samphan, the former Khmer Rouge minister of foreign affairs, wrote his autobiography. The book enraged the whole Cambodian community. He said that he did not really know what was actually happening during the darkest period of the Khmer Rouge regime. He tried to persuade the public that he had not been involved in the Killing Fields. I could hardly believe that this former Khmer Rouge leader, who had received a doctorate degree in France, could be so morally bankrupt. He had no courage to face what he had actually done to his own people, and it seemed as if his moral conscience had been eroded by his fear of losing face. How could he reconcile himself with the Killing Fields survivors? There will be no reconciliation in our country while this leader fails to recognize the reality of his dreadful leadership, warped perspective and irresponsible moral conduct.

There are several former Khmer Rouge leaders still living peacefully in Cambodia, but most survivors of the Killing Fields expect them to be tried for genocide. Whether fair trials are a possibility, with the current level of corruption in government, remains to be seen. Personally, I believe that if a fair trial became possible, it would not only affect the remaining Khmer Rouge leaders, but would also bring to light the outside forces that were involved in supporting the evil regime. Years ago, I saw a young boy crying loudly because his father could not catch the moon for him. He saw the reflection of the moon in the water, and his father did not know what to do, because the moon was beyond his reach. Centuries ago, a prophet wrote, 'We look for justice, but find none' (Isaiah 59:11), and this same cry for justice among Cambodians has also gone unheard.

I don't believe the remaining Khmer Rouge leaders will ever make a public confession or ask for forgiveness from their victims, so national reconciliation will be impossible to achieve. There is only one way forward, and that is for the gospel of the grace of God, and his free forgiveness through the atoning death of Jesus on the cross, to be preached throughout our land. When that happens and Cambodians learn to open their hearts to the healing that is available for them through receiving the redemptive love of God, then progress towards reconciliation could take place. I believe that only this message of forgiveness through Christ will succeed in healing the wounds of our nation.

INTRODUCTION

A brief glimpse into the political history of Cambodia

I have several good friends from Singapore who have come to visit churches in my home town. They tell me that forty years ago, Cambodia was a rich and prosperous country and that they learned a lot from it. None of them ever thought that our land would become 'the Killing Fields'. Similarly, after I had spoken at a leadership conference in New Haven, Connecticut, people asked me how such a beautiful country could end in such desolation. Let me try to paint a picture of the political history of Cambodia, which I hope will show that Cambodians need to learn to deal with forgiveness and healing. I think it may also be helpful to people from other countries where the political situation has some similarities to that of Cambodia.

To gain an in-depth understanding of the minds of Cambodians who have been psychologically traumatized, it is necessary to examine the legacies of the civil wars and the nature of the political violence that occurred when Cambodia gained independence from the French in 1953. From that time to the present day, Cambodia has gone through many political changes.

Each change seemed to inflict more psychological trauma on the Cambodians, as every one of these periods brought out the evil side of human nature: wars, crimes, political assassinations, corruption, executions, torture, kidnappings, incest, rape, and domestic violence. The product of these years was a people sickened and exhausted by such evil, longing for an end to the bloodshed in the country and for the possibility of peace.

The Sihanouk regime (1953 to 1970)

Cambodia was once known as the 'Land of Paradise' in South-east Asia. Its natives, the Mon-Khmers, led a peaceful, harmonious existence, cultivating rice in the countryside. However, in the latter half of the twentieth century things began to change. In 1941 Prince Norodom Sihanouk was elected as king of Cambodia and managed to bring the country to full independence by 1954. A year later he relinquished the throne to his father, entered the political arena and became both Prime Minister and Head of State. During this time, he tried to keep Cambodia out of the wars being fought in neighbouring countries. He was reasonably successful in dealing with external political pressures but failed to manage internal political factions.

As Sihanouk struggled to maintain control over his supporters, he met with opposition from the Khmer Rouge leftists (also known as Red Khmers or Khmer Communists) who were led by Pol Pot. Educated in France[1] along with Ieng Sary and Khieu Samphan, the Khmer Rouge (or KR) leaders hid in the jungles and there learned guerrilla tactics and prepared to overthrow Sihanouk. In early 1970, the king was dethroned and the monarchy was abolished. Sihanouk's regime itself did not create terror, nor did it inflict pain on society. These came when the civil war was birthed. Seanglim Bit draws this conclusion about Sihanouk's regime:

> At a juncture in history where Cambodia might have developed the foundations for a democratic society, what evolved instead was a system that denied basic human rights. The price of dissent became possible death, disappearance, flight to escape certain execution, sanctions against family members, or at a minimum, public humiliation and loss of employment.[2]

The Lon Nol regime (1970 to 1975)

A Khmer republic was established under the leadership of General Lon Nol, who was supported by the United States. After Sihanouk was deposed, he went to China where he allied himself with his former enemies, the Khmer Rouge, to try to regain control of Cambodia. He became the head of state for the Khmer Rouge, but had no actual power over their soldiers.[3]

Meanwhile, the republican government had grown totally corrupt; society became chaotic, and this provoked hatred, anger and rancour among Cambodians who had formerly supported the monarchy. Many who hated such corruption joined the Khmer Rouge to fight against this government, and civil war raged throughout the country. The republican government asked the American military to bomb the Khmer Rouge soldiers in the jungles and countryside. Kiernan indicates that by March 1973, the bombardment had spread west to envelop the whole country. Around Phnom Penh, 3,000 civilians were killed in three weeks in air-raids on villages. Refugees swarmed into the capital from target areas, and as much as half the population was killed or maimed in the bombing raids. Later, the US bombardment intensified to reach a level of 3,600 tons per day.[4]

Some elderly people who survived the bombs recall that government soldiers sometimes marched into villages and arrested men, accusing them of being involved with the Khmer Rouge. These men were brutally tortured and forced to reveal the hiding-place of the Khmer Rouge. In other villages, soldiers marched in to finish off those who had survived the bombing, even killing innocent children. One Cambodian survivor lamented, 'The bombers may have killed some Communists, but they also killed everyone else too.'[5] The actions of the soldiers only created hatred and anger among the people in the countryside. They were given no choice except to join the Khmer Rouge and fight back. Brutally traumatized by the government soldiers, they vowed they would never forget what had been done to the people in the villages. They waited for an opportunity to take vengeance; this was a sign of the escalating violence in society.

The more the government soldiers attacked the countryside, the more the Khmer Rouge fought back, shelling cities and towns, and planting plastic explosives in public places such as movie theatres and markets, killing more people. By late 1974, the government had weakened and its soldiers had lost hope of defending their country, as most of the rural areas were under the control of the Khmer Rouge. On 17 April 1975, the Khmer Rouge soldiers captured the whole country. It was estimated that over the five years of Lon Nol's regime, more than half a million civilians were killed and hundreds of thousands were handicapped.

The Khmer Rouge regime (1975 to 1979)

On 17th April 1975 the Khmer Rouge made history with their victory over capitalism, as they ended five years of civil war. Across the nation, cheerful Cambodians cele- brated because they thought that the war was over and that they would live in peace and prosperity. They were so happy that both the Khmer Rouge and ordinary citi- zens jumped for joy and danced in the streets. Khieu Samphan announced that the country would be an inde- pendent, peaceful, neutral, non-aligned Cambodia with territorial integrity.[6] Instead, this once peaceful land became the place of the Killing Fields as Khmer Rouge propaganda ploughed through it, leaving behind chaos, suffering and death.

Suddenly, things were turned upside down. According to Kiernan, Pol Pot made eight declarations that were to become law:[7]

- Evacuate the people from all the towns and cities.
- Abolish all markets.
- Abolish the Lon Nol regime's currency and withhold the revolutionary currency that had been printed.
- Defrock all Buddhist monks and put them to work growing rice.
- Execute all the leaders of the Lon Nol regime, begin- ning with the most senior ones.
- Establish high-level cooperatives throughout the country, with communal eating.
- Expel the entire Vietnamese minority population.

• Dispatch troops to the borders, particularly the Vietnamese border.

People in the towns never expected that the Khmer Rouge would carry out these plans, and most Khmer Rouge soldiers did not know of the plan to evacuate the towns. Only a few of the top leaders actually knew, and the action was taken a few days after they had won control of the country. In reality, these plans contradicted the propaganda they had been spreading when they were trying to liberate Cambodia from the Lon Nol government. How did people respond to the evacuation from the towns? Some of those I interviewed recall that the evacuation process was a total shock to them. Young Khmer Rouge soldiers, with little or no education, crudely ordered the people to leave their towns for three days and not take anything with them, except enough food for those three days. A survivor recalls the terror she experienced then:

Suddenly, five young Khmer Rouge soldiers bounded through the doorway with their rifles pointed straight at us. The blood drained from my face and I went cold with terror. Then they stared at us and ordered us to leave the town immediately. 'We won't harm you, but you must leave immediately.' My family was shocked to hear such an order so we started asking questions, but they suddenly shouted angrily, 'Now, if you do not want to listen, don't say that we have no compassion. We will give you an hour to leave and it is up to you to decide. However, you must be responsible for your own actions.' Our fear returned greater than before, and we agreed to leave immediately. The sight of their rifles pointed straight at our hearts left us in no doubt as to the consequences of disobeying these Khmer Rouge soldiers.[8]

The evacuation caused deep terror and many were traumatized as they wondered why the soldiers treated them with no mercy. The *New York Times* reported:

> Some twelve weeks after the Communist entry into Phnom Penh and the forced exodus on foot of millions of urban Cambodians to distant country areas, a veil of silence still cloaks the full horror of what happened – with the worst yet to come in predicted deaths from hunger and disease. The agony and degradation that followed may never be fully known. Tens of thousands are believed to have fallen by the wayside, victims of hunger, thirst, exhaustion and disease including a spreading cholera epidemic.[9]

Some people were separated from their families in the process of evacuation and never saw their relatives again. One man recalls in tears how, as an eight-year-old boy, he was separated from his parents. He shouted loudly for them in the first two days after the separation. It was futile. He could not get anything to eat and did not know where to go. He just kept walking along with a huge crowd of people unknown to him. Even now, almost thirty years after the separation, he still does not know what happened to his parents and relatives. He concludes that Khmer Rouge soldiers killed all of them. Otherwise, they would have come to look for him or news about his family would have come to him.

Another survivor told of her four traumatic days during the evacuation. Her nineteen-year-old brother, who had been ill with malaria for several months, was very weak. As they were forced out of Phnom Penh, he tried to keep up with the family, but soon stumbled and fell. Three Khmer Rouge soldiers pulled him from the supporting arms of his family and shot him dead. They pushed the others onward, leaving her brother's body on the road; those who followed stepped over the corpse. Her family and other people were forced to continue walking for about a month. She saw people dying day after day, and she had to walk around the bodies on the road.[10]

Soon after the soldiers had emptied the cities and towns, they went on to implement other plans. They invited all those who had been associated with the republican government to appear before them. High-ranking army officers, government officials and intellectuals were all summoned; they were told to study the doctrines of the new regime if they wanted to cooperate with the government of the future. All these people were anxious to retain their positions of authority, so they accepted the invitation but never returned. All were killed. This was the first taste of the brutal mentality of the Khmer Rouge. No one would be able to rationalize this terrible tragedy.

Charitthy Him writes in her memoirs that during the KR regime, the life of Cambodia's villagers was worse than that of pigs.[11] Her father and her uncles were sent to study the doctrines of the new government and never came back. She was only nine years old when her father was killed. She recalls the shock when her father did not come home one evening:

> I went to look for Pa, but figured I had time to get a bowl of rice and soup to ease my growling stomach. With a bowl of food in my hand, I ran looking for him in the house while

shoving a few bites in my mouth. I saw only my mother and my sisters and aunts. 'Mother, where did Pa [father] go?' I asked, feeling scared. 'They brought ox-carts to take your father and uncles.' My mother speaks softly as she sits on the floor folding clothes. I stormed out, running down the stairs, one hand gripping my rice bowl, the other clutching the railing. I wanted to catch up with Pa to see him again. I ran to the path behind Kong Houng's house, but he's nowhere to be found! My uncles are gone too, no ox-carts and no one is there. My mouth no longer chews the food, but simply releases a sound of immense sadness. Never before have I felt so much pain inside my body, my chest, my eyes and my throat; grief encompasses every cell, touches every limb, every organ. For Pa has never left me for more than a day, now he's gone.[15]

After her father was taken away, life became hard. She was forced to do hard labour but was given little food to eat. Her family was treated brutally by the soldiers and she was not allowed to complain about the work or the lack of food – otherwise they would exterminate her family.

Sophea (not her real name) was twenty years old when the evacuation took place. She recalls the arrest of a friend. Two soldiers arrested her and took her into the jungle for execution; all Sophea heard was her friend's scream from the jungle. She describes life after that event as one full of despair:

At that time, I did not know when my turn would arrive. Fear and terror crept into my life every night. I knew that Khmer Rouge soldiers sneaked under my house to listen to my family – if we said anything bad about them, they would arrest and then execute us. Some time after that I got married and moved to live in another village with my husband.

About one year after that, I met a friend who lived in the village where my parents were. She asked to talk to me privately. She said, 'I would like to tell you something about your family; they were killed a few months ago.' As soon as I heard that, I fainted. When I revived, I felt as though my spirit had left me [meaning loss of consciousness]. Now, twenty-five years after that trauma, I still have nightmares. I could not overcome the terror I experienced during the darkest period in my life.

A former general who recently resigned from the military also experienced trauma during the Khmer Rouge regime:

One night, my mother, younger sister and brother and I were arrested, because my father was a high-ranking military officer. Khmer Rouge soldiers tied our arms behind our backs so tightly I could feel the rope biting into my flesh. They told us that they would destroy us. Fear was so great it threatened to take over my life. Half-way into the jungle, my mother fainted and fell down. My younger brother and I took a risk by escaping into the dark jungle even though we could not see anything. We were lucky. We survived in the jungle for almost a year but my life was coloured with anger and vengeance. In early 1979, Vietnamese soldiers liberated us from the Khmer Rouge regime. I sent my younger brother to live with my relatives while I joined the soldiers fighting against the remaining Khmer Rouge. I went back to the village where I lost my mother and sister and finished off those who had killed them. I fought almost one thousand battles, but now I am no longer a general. I can hardly cope with the terror of what happened to me twenty-seven years ago. Nightmares bother me a lot these days. I wish I could abolish these memories from my head. Now, I cannot function properly.

My normal way of thinking becomes disrupted by terrible memories.

Rema (not her real name), who was about fifteen years old at the time, remembers how her father, a high-ranking officer of the Lon Nol regime, was arrested and taken into the jungle late one evening. She followed behind to see what the soldiers would do. They took her father to a pit and made him kneel in front of what was to be his grave. Then they clubbed him from behind with a hoe. It was the last time she saw him. Although it is more than twenty-five years since that traumatic event, she cannot get rid of the painful memory. She does not want to remember it, but finds it impossible to remove it from her mind.

The Khmer Rouge regime, lasting three years, eight months and twenty days, succeeded in accomplishing the eight points of Pol Pot's plan. The Cambodian people, especially those who are now more than forty years old, were exposed to severe psychological trauma during this dark period. In my interviews with Cambodian Killing Field survivors they indicated that they had lost at least one relative, usually the male head of the family.

The Khmer Rouge also attempted to restructure the family. Children and parents were separated; other children, many of them illiterate, were put into positions of power over adults. The youths were sent far away from home to do hard work, with little food to eat. Husbands and wives were separated and forced to work hard in the rice fields from morning till late evening. If they complained, they were executed.

The Khmer Rouge also carried out 'ethnic cleansing' against the Chams (Cambodian Muslims), the Chinese, the Vietnamese, the Thais, the Laotians and others living within the Cambodian borders.[13] They treated the Chinese and the Chams badly, but they hated the Vietnamese the most. This stems from a long history of conflict between the two races. Thus the Khmer Rouge enlisted the Vietnamese in their plan. City-dwellers, because they generally had fairer skin, were accused of being Chinese, even though not all people from the cities were ethnic Chinese. The treatment of these city-dwellers was brutal, and they were often called 'slaves of the capitalists' or 'worthless people'.

The Khmer Rouge composed a saying that was very powerful and frightening: 'If we keep you, we gain nothing, but if we kill you, we lose nothing.' If they used this saying against anyone in the daytime, that person would disappear in the night. All my interviewees reported that whenever they heard this saying, they would not be able to sleep. They were so frightened, wondering who would be killed in the night. The soldiers would come knocking on the door and invite the person to whom they had spoken the saying to go with them and 'learn new doctrines'. That person would never come back to the family again. As soon as night arrived, the interviewees would feel the chill of fear and terror creeping back into their lives. In effect, this saying became a form of psychological torture that crippled everyone who heard it, especially the city-dwellers.

Fear of death dominated our lives, which were lived out under the non-stop watchfulness of the Khmer Rouge soldiers. There was torture and execution every day. Without doubt, such emotional and psychological trauma remains in the survivors today. Is such psychological damage beyond repair? P. Yathay, who survived the Killing Fields too, wrote in his autobiography:

> The tragedy of Cambodia has not yet run its course, nor will it for generations. Millions have died, a culture has vanished. The personal consequences of such a tragedy are incalculable, comparable only to the destruction wrought by the Black Death in Europe, by the Jewish Holocaust, and by the Stalinist Gulag.[14]

Seanglim Bit has pointed out: 'Directly associated with the use of intentional violence to promote the Khmer Rouge goals was the use of fear and terror to instil passive acceptance and compliance of the population held hostage.'[15] Anyone who complained against the Khmer Rouge would disappear forever. Many were killed as an example and in order to intimidate others, as violence was used to psychologically pressure people. How would Cambodians live with this intimidation and terror?

A woman shared her experience of powerlessness when she saw the Khmer Rouge soldiers kill her friends in front of her as an example to her. She felt frozen and paralysed; her knees trembled for months afterwards and she felt as though the muscles of her legs were lifeless. Great fear took over her life and for years, after all she had seen happen to her friends, she felt continually sick and depressed.

A man who saw his family killed by the Khmer Rouge described his fear and anger as an electric shock. It crippled his life for years. Sometimes, he felt as though it might explode inside him. He did not know how to erase his anger and fear.

Another traumatic experience that people reported

was the paralysis that fear and terror bring, especially in the middle of the night. When the Khmer Rouge wanted to kill anyone, they often came to knock on the victim's door in the middle of the night. They would take the victim to the jungle immediately and kill him or her. Bit observes:

> It is the memory of overwhelming fear and unrelenting terror that survivors recalled in graphic details long after the threat of immediate violence has subsided. Cambodian survivors have experienced powerlessness in its ultimate form. At a personal level, unrelenting fear leads to a sense of hopelessness, inertia, and for some, the lack of will to attempt to improve one's condition.[16]

Not many people in the West can ever imagine how horrific were the experiences endured by the Cambodians in the last half century. Most in the West have heard the story of the Holocaust, but few have heard much about the Killing Fields – how the Khmer Rouge soldiers came to power and killed more than two million innocent Cambodians. Even if they have heard something about the Killing Fields, they cannot begin to understand what Cambodians went through. Rather, the media seem to have minimized the brutality and evil done by the Khmer Rouge soldiers.

The Communist regime (1979 to 1991)

In early 1979, Vietnamese soldiers liberated Cambodia from the evil regime of the Khmer Rouge. Another Communist government was established, now with the support of the Vietnamese government. Cambodians became exposed to yet another form of psychological trauma. A few months after the invasion, this new government lost control. They could not do anything to prevent the so-called 'street justice', which involved killing people of the Khmer Rouge regime such as village chiefs, group leaders, commune chiefs and secret agents. These were stoned, chopped or kicked to death by angry Killing Fields survivors. The Vietnamese soldiers could do nothing with these angry people. They could not control them nor judge who was right or wrong; they just closed their eyes.

At this stage, Cambodians were propelled along by the saying, 'Fish and ants take turns eating each other', meaning that when the water level is up, the fish eat the ants, and when the water level is down, the ants eat the fish. This saying took deep root in the Cambodians' souls as they looked for every opportunity to take revenge. Thus when the Khmer Rouge soldiers defeated the Republic, they killed most of the Republican soldiers. When the Vietnamese army took over from the Khmer Rouge, people killed many Khmer Rouge soldiers. This 'street justice', with its relentless round of killings, brought more psychological trauma to Cambodian society.

Even though the Vietnamese army had pushed the remaining Khmer Rouge soldiers to the Thai–Cambodian border, the war did not stop. It spread across the countryside and along the border. Two other political parties – the Khmer People's National Liberation Front (KPNLF), led by Son Sann, an exiled former Cambodian prime minister, and the FUNCINPEC party, led by King Sihanouk – sprang up near the border, with the intention of fighting the Vietnamese invasion. These two parties were supported by America and Europe. By early

1982, both forces had launched fierce attacks on the Cambodian government soldiers and the Vietnamese army. Khmer Rouge soldiers also helped in the attack. According to a young former Khmer Rouge soldier (an interviewee) who went to study in China before the fall of the Khmer Rouge regime, about 5,000 soldiers were called back to fight the Vietnamese army in Cambodia. Their tactics of war were not to gain control of the cities or towns, but to paralyse, then attack and pull out, so that those in the local government could not sleep or function properly. This tactic only created more traumatic experiences for the Cambodian people.

This long civil war was extremely demoralizing. People in the countryside were the victims of war on both sides. Several interviewees in the province of Siem Reap said that during the period from 1981 to 1989, people went through several unimaginably traumatic events. When the Vietnamese and Cambodian government soldiers came into the villages, they arrested most of the young men, accusing them of being involved with the Khmer Rouge, or with Son Sann's or Sihanouk's guerrillas, or of hiding them, and they put these young men in prison without investigation. After the government soldiers withdrew, the guerrillas came in and accused the people of supporting the Vietnamese soldiers. Thus, both sides psychologically tortured the people in the countryside.

A present Cambodian government soldier reported that during the conflict between the government and the guerrillas in 1987, near their village he had arrested two young men whom he suspected of being spies for the guerrillas. He brought them to his commander for interrogation. A few hours afterwards, he learned that his commander had killed those two poor men. Three days later, the parents of the two victims came to look for the bodies. This soldier admitted now that if the terrible civil war had not been stopped, more Cambodians would have become psychologically crippled, especially those in the countryside. Many lives were lost in that war. It is estimated that more than half a million people died – including soldiers from both sides and civilians – while many others were handicapped.

Between 1985 and 1987, the Cambodian government implemented a new strategy to prevent attacks by the three guerrilla groups. They forced people from the cities and towns to cut down the forests along the Thai–Cambodian border and plant landmines instead, so that the guerrillas could not cross over to attack Cambodia. Thousands of innocent lives were lost this way. Some died from stepping on the mines, some died from sicknesses such as malaria, and others died while trying to escape either to Thailand or to the refugee camps because they had got lost in the forests. For some survivors, this government strategy became one of the most brutal and traumatic events they had experienced. One saying goes like this: 'When you go, you get a ride on a military truck but when you come back, you get a ride in a bowl.' People were forced into military trucks and were taken away to cut down the forests. And if they died on duty, the body would be cremated, with the ash typically put in a bowl to be brought back to the family. This was very common in Cambodian culture, as the family could not afford to bring the body home. It was usually very far and it could take at least five days for the trip home. Families who stayed at home waiting for their loved ones to return from the forests suffered from sleeplessness, nightmares and worry.

Refugee camps

In early 1979, the Khmer Rouge regime was taken over by the Vietnamese Communists. Soon afterwards, people were allowed to return home to join their surviving relatives. Some – especially those who had formerly been Khmer Rouge soldiers – did not go home but instead escaped to the Thai–Cambodian border because they feared the new Communist government. They were also motivated by basic physical needs. After the wars, apart from the psychological trauma, millions were sick and there were no medicines available. It was believed that medical help at the border was excellent and widely available to any refugee. Making a trip to a refugee camp was very difficult and dangerous, but those who were ill had no choice left and took the risk.

By late 1979, masses of Cambodian refugees began streaming towards the Thai border. Their arrival overwhelmed the small relief and resettlement efforts, and the response from the Thai government was apathetic. They had no compassion for the refugees. They gathered them together and forced them to return to Cambodia over Preah Vihear Mountain. The mountain, about 400 kilometres from Phnom Penh, slopes gently on the Thai side, but the refugees faced danger as they had to negotiate the steep drop into Cambodia. Many died on the way; others died of starvation before they reached towns; others were robbed and killed by Khmer Rouge guerrillas. One man described his journey back home as a trip to hell. His wife was robbed and killed by a small group of Khmer Rouge soldiers while he watched helplessly, unable to do anything to protect her.

From 1979 to 1985, more than one million Cambodians escaped to Thai refugee camps. The Thai government was not pleased about the camps being set up in its territory. The Thais pushed the unfortunate refugees to the border, and Vietnamese soldiers pushed them back into Thai territory. The United Nations, the Red Cross and Western voluntary relief agencies set up these camps. The refugees did not stay long. Some intended to leave for third countries while others went to join the guerrillas to fight against the Vietnamese soldiers occupying Cambodia. On the way to the camps, many people endangered their lives as they walked through a countryside littered with landmines and booby traps. Crossing the battle zones was dangerous too. Even walking across unfamiliar fields could be a matter of life and death. Some never arrived, as they were arrested by government soldiers and put in prison for years. Others were attacked by guerrillas.

Life in the camps was a terrible existence and both the Cambodian soldiers and the Thai army treated the refugees badly. In late 1984, the Cambodian government, with the Vietnamese army, launched a fierce attack to destroy all the camps along the Thai–Cambodian border. The refugees all along the border were displaced again and again.

A transition to democracy (from 1991 to 2004)

In 1991, the Paris Peace Agreement was signed. All refugees along the border were to return to their homeland, and all Cambodian political parties outside

Cambodia were to return to Phnom Penh to prepare for the first national elections, which took place in 1993. By the end of 1991, the Vietnamese soldiers had totally withdrawn from Cambodia.

Before the first national election took place, the country was very much in chaos. Soldiers from different political parties could not get along with each other and society became lawless. Anybody, even a taxi driver, could have a gun. Robberies and kidnappings were the nightmares of the rich and also for those who had gone to Cambodia to help the traumatized people. Shootings and killings happened every day.

The FUNCINPEC political party won the 1993 election, but the Cambodian People's Party (CPP) was not willing to give up power. Consequently each of the two parties appointed its own prime minister to run the same country. This did not bring peace, but rather chaos and trauma. Cambodians believe that one mountain cannot be ruled by two tigers, for there can be no peace that way. This saying was proved to be true as, in July 1997, the second prime minister, Hun Sen, ousted the first prime minister, Ranariddh. During this period, fighting broke out in Phnom Penh; people were killed and looting became widespread in the city. The psychological impact on the city-dwellers was very severe.

During the first and second national elections, Cambodia was totally infected by the disease of corruption. The second national election took place in 1998. This time the CPP won the election, but did not gain enough seats to form a government by itself. Therefore they had to join with the FUNCINPEC party. The third national election took place in 2003 and the CPP won again, but still lacked the number of seats needed to form the government. Again, they had to marry with the FUNCIPEC party. The political situation is now more stable, but the peace is an uneasy one. Corruption has become a way of life for most Cambodian people. The government has agreed with the leaders of the nations that contribute financially to Cambodia that they need to stop the corruption, but unfortunately they have not succeeded. It is like a disease that spreads out to eat at the moral conscience of Cambodians. If this disease is not treated soon, it will infect the whole society and bring economic crisis and social disruption.

The Cambodian people do not have full freedom yet. The concept of democracy has not been absorbed into their society, and I believe it will take many more years to implement real democracy. People do not have freedom to speak from their hearts and knowledge. Some people who oppose or criticize the government's view are arrested and put in jail. Opposition party supporters are still killed from time to time. The government tries to use its court system and military force to manipulate those who oppose them.

The weakness of democracy in Cambodia is due to the people's failure to stand together to fight for freedom. After the dark period of the Khmer Rouge regime, Cambodians were psychologically crippled. They had seen enough killing in their lives and they just do not want to face psychological traumas again. They might not be happy with the government, but the fear of being arrested cripples them, so they cannot fight for freedom. If the country continues like this, Cambodia will become the second Myanmar. Democracy will never be realized, but it will die with tragic consequences.

Gun control has not been effective, so robberies and

kidnappings are still good business for bad people. The government still struggles to control both, but the people still practise 'street justice'. A robber arrested by the police and put into prison is safe, but if the people catch him first, they torture him to death before the police arrive.

After such a history of political violence and wars, lasting from 1953 to 2004, it is undeniable that many Cambodians have suffered psychological trauma. One of the most traumatic periods was that from 1975 to 1979, a war orchestrated by Pol Pot, the Khmer Rouge leader. More than two million Cambodians died of starvation, disease and overwork, or by execution. Survivors of the Killing Fields have experienced the deaths of loved ones, witnessed and experienced torture, gone on forced migration and faced the loss of all personal possessions. Even now, twenty-five years after the Killing Fields, Cambodians are still not interested in talking about what they have gone through. They live in silence, but they need to learn how to deal with the unwanted legacies of psychological trauma, and also to forgive. I am very much concerned for the future of our nation. If their trauma is left untreated, the whole of Cambodian society will face immense psychological disruption. As Cambodian people, we need to address this issue.

Notes

1. David Chandler, *A History of Cambodia*, San Francisco: Westview Press, 1992.
2. Seanglim Bit, *The Warrior Heritage: A Psychological Perspective of Trauma*, El Cerrito, California: Seanglim, 1991, p. 78.

3. Himm, Sokreaksa, *The Tears of my Soul*, Oxford: Monarch Books 2003, p. 10.
4. Ben Kiernan, *The Pol Pot Regime*, Chiang Mai: Silkworm Books, 1996, p. 21.
5. Kiernan, *The Pol Pot Regime*, p. 21.
6. Kiernan, *The Pol Pot Regime*, p. 54.
7. Kiernan, *The Pol Pot Regime*, p. 55.
8. Var Hong Ashe, *From Phnom Penh to Paradise: Escape from the Killing Fields*, London: Hodder & Stoughton, 1988, p. 27.
9. Chanrithy Him, *When Broken Glass Floats*, New York: W. W. Northon & Co., 2000, p. 106.
10. Kamm, Henry, *Cambodia: report from a stricken land*, pub: Arcade Pub, New York, c 1998, p. 125
11. Him, *When Broken Glass Floats*, p. 89.
12. Him, *When Broken Glass Floats*, p. 89.

13. Kiernan, *The Pol Pot Regime*, p. 57.
14. P. Yathay, *Stay Alive, My Son*, London: Bloomsbury Publishing, 1987, pp. 237–38.
15. Bit, *The Warrior Heritage*, p. 85.
16. Bit, *The Warrior Heritage*, p. 85.

CHAPTER ONE

SEARCHING FOR
MY FAMILY'S KILLERS

The will to forgive

I was brought up in a large family in Siemreap, a pleasant town in northern Cambodia where mango, coconut, guava and papaya trees grew. There were beautiful wild flowers, and in swampy areas, perhaps the lotus flower was the most beautiful of all. A small river ran gently through the town and many houses were built along its banks. People fetched water from the river to use in their houses and to water their plants. Our house was about 150 metres from the river, so I used to go to swimming every afternoon, and sometimes I went fishing with my older brothers.

With eleven brothers and sisters, I was part of a large, happy and united family. My father was a teacher so we lived in a comfortable home with a large garden in a quiet and spacious area of the town. I had lots of fun playing with my older and younger brothers and, being in the middle of the family, I thought I had the best of everything! I knew how to relate to my older and younger siblings. Sometimes I chose to be an older brother so I could have authority over the younger ones, and at other times I preferred to be a younger brother so I could be more manipulative with the older ones. But life was a happy experience and I was good at communicating with all of them.

My parents were Buddhists, so they took us all to worship in the pagoda from time to time, and in the home we were brought up with good moral values and discipline. We rose early, at 5:00 a.m., to help with cleaning the house and washing our clothes, and then after breakfast we went to school. My older siblings actually were up earlier than I was to attend to their studies because our parents thought we could assimilate new information better when our minds were fresh. At 6:30 a.m. we younger ones walked along the dusty roads to our school, which was nearby. My older siblings went to a different school further away, so they went on their bicycles. School started at 7:00 a.m. and we usually came home for lunch. My mother left home early as she had a business in the market. She was very astute and earned more than my father.

With both parents working, life was busy, but we always had time together as a family. My father motivated us to aim for higher education. He had a special saying: 'Man who is without knowledge is always brought down by what he does not understand.' Even though his family had been farmers, he had always wanted to teach, and he succeeded in obtaining a teaching certificate from a French school. At that time this was a highly regarded qualification. I am sure he never dreamed that his good education would eventually lead to his untimely death at the hands of illiterate, uneducated peasant soldiers. In our free time, my father took me fishing, and this was something I always looked forward to, as I loved his company and felt so happy and secure with him.

In those early, happy days I never thought this joy would end so suddenly. Khmer Rouge soldiers, who had taken over our once peaceful country, forced us at gunpoint to leave our home. After months of suffering, hardship, near starvation and torture, my much-loved family members and I were rounded up by the cruel soldiers and ordered to stand round an open grave. They began to club each one of us with hoes and blunt instruments and, one by one, we fell into the grave, lifeless. Supposing we were all dead, the soldiers left the grave before they thought of filling it in. Perhaps they were searching for others to kill. I was in that grave too, but the evil soldiers had not succeeded in killing me. God had his hand on me, because I regained consciousness as the evening fell. Then began the awful experience of trying to climb out from under the bodies of my beloved family. I was injured but struggled to disentangle myself and climb out of that grave. I was just thirteen years old when I stood by that terrible open grave, wondering how I could possibly survive, and whether there could ever be any future for me.

In my first book, *The Tears of My Soul* (published by Monarch in 2003), I was eager to share the details of my experience of forgiveness, but was discouraged by the influence of Western society, whereby everything has to be theorized and scientifically proven. What I actually wanted to share in my book had nothing to do with scientific or theoretical concepts. As I was in the process of trying to write, I remembered two experiences I'd had in Canada, and because of these I became convinced that writing about this terrible event would help others to forgive after hurtful experiences in their own lives. Writing in detail on forgiveness from my own experience would be costly, but I felt this message must be written down to help others who struggle with past traumatic experiences.

After becoming a Christian, I searched hungrily for the full meaning of forgiveness. I desperately wanted to know everything about this subject. I spent a lot of time reading books about it, but I never felt satisfied. I went to church and heard preachers preaching on forgiveness and I thought the messages were wonderful, but I found myself struggling to apply them to my life. I remembered one preacher who had preached on forgiveness from the parable of the prodigal son. After he had finished preaching, I approached him and asked, 'What does it mean to forgive? What is its significance?' He did not answer right away. He looked at me with a smiling face but then he stopped smiling. My heart beat faster. I thought that he was about to tell me the answer to my question. Instead, he asked very bluntly, 'Were you sleeping while I was preaching?' Then he walked away. I left the church feeling confused and blamed myself for being silly. Perhaps I had approached him at the wrong time or the question was not appropriate. He may have wanted me to reflect on his message by myself. But, in a sense, I felt rejected by him and lost.

Later, another preacher spoke on forgiveness, using the same story. After he finished, I approached him and asked him the same question that I had asked the other preacher. His response was similar. He smiled at me, but he did not answer. He gave me his business card and said, 'Give me a call some time and we will talk about it.'

I left that church deep in thought, but these two experiences discouraged me from writing in detail on forgiveness in my first book, because I thought I was not qualified to do so.

Another deterrent to my writing in North American society was the prevalent perception that, in order to speak on forgiveness, one has to be a famous theologian or a well-known preacher, otherwise no one would listen to the message. I am neither a theologian nor a preacher, so I felt I had nothing to offer. I left my writing on forgiveness in a kind of deep, silent therapy. What I actually did in my first book was to share very briefly on forgiveness. In my heart, there was no doubt that I had forgiven my family's killers, but my writing seemed to suggest that I had some unfinished business, because I had written so little on forgiveness. Many readers were left wondering whether I had actually forgiven my family's killers, while others asked whether I had been reconciled with them. These are very significant questions.

What I had left behind – the deep, silent therapy – was awakened after my first trip to promote *The Tears of My Soul* in the UK. Two significant experiences motivated me to pursue this writing. Firstly, after speaking in Northern Ireland, an elderly lady approached me, gave me a hug and said, 'I cannot imagine how you could forgive your family's killers. I have been a Christian most of my life, but I cannot forgive friends who have hurt me. Your message of forgiveness today has led me to see a small glimpse of freedom for my life. Could you write in detail from your own experience on how you could forgive your family's killers so that I can learn how to forgive from your experience?'

I was speechless and didn't know what to say to her. I

wished I could tell her more, but I felt inadequate because the influence of Western mentality was very fresh in my mind and I was too shy, so she left me and I saw tears running down her face. I could tell that she was deeply hurt and had been carrying a deep root of bitterness in her life. She did not know how to remove it, nor did she know where to find freedom in forgiveness. In reality, I had once been like her. When I could not forgive my family's killers, I had lived with the bitterness in my life for many years. I did not know how she felt, but I believed her life was a cesspool of bitterness and pain.

On the second occasion, just after I had spoken at a community church in Scotland, a veteran pastor led me out of his church and said to me, 'Your testimony and message of forgiveness puts me to shame. I have never heard such a message in my life, and I've been a pastor for more than twenty-five years, but I could not forgive my wife after she left me. Your message has touched my heart deeply and given me a taste of forgiveness. Could you write in detail about how you were able to forgive your family's killers? People in the Western world need to learn from you how to forgive.'

I was stunned. At first, I thought that he was being sarcastic, because I had often heard pastors and church leaders encourage me to forgive my family's killers. Now, a pastor was asking me to help him to forgive. As he held back tears I realized that he was serious, but I didn't know what more to say to him, so I gave him a hug. I felt very warm holding him silently in my arms. Neither of us had any words to say. Finally, he led me back inside his church where many people approached me and offered words of encouragement about what I had shared. Leaving his church with his words planted firmly in my mind, I realized that my motivation to write on forgiveness had been confirmed, and that I must not keep silent. However, after I returned to Cambodia, I slipped into a deep lethargy; I lacked the discipline and would have preferred to cook for a whole village rather than sit down at the computer and write a book! However, thankfully, I received several emails from readers encouraging me to write an experience-based book. Many of them had been through difficult times like me. One lady, for example, said:

> I have had difficulties forgiving in my past ... I work on it every day. The bad memories come back so I have to give this to God every day. Your lessons of forgiveness have given me the strength to carry on sending love to the people I have had 'learning experiences' with. I know that without these past hurts I would not be the person I am today.

Another person wrote of a personal experience of sexual abuse:

> I often struggle with fear and till recently with a need for justice. I am exhausted by my struggle and often feel like giving in. I was experiencing just such a day when God led me to pick up a copy of your book. On opening it I was stunned by the integrity of your honesty and identified with the intensity of your questions about your struggle. Although I don't think I have ever been in fear of my life, my abuser threatened me with humiliation, the demolition of the life of any witnesses I may find, that my story would be ridiculed, disregarded ...
> As I read your book I was relieved to find an individual who has suffered and survived - a person who holds out the

promise of God's power to save and heal. Sometimes I can hardly believe this for myself and my hope flounders ... I think that the fact that you struggled with the disparity between the theory and practice of forgiveness and yet still advocated it was really important to me. I too have come across many people who talk about forgiveness as if it is something I could give without cost or impact to my own life. I have been irritated by such responses for years.

I was really encouraged by your simple statement about forgiveness, that 'Forgiveness has released me from the emotional torment that burned within me for years, and now my heart is lighter and my spirit has peace.' Through this and another small testimony affirming the power of forgiveness I recognize that I need to forgive those who have hurt, damaged and neglected me. I am pleased to say that God has led me into forgiving those people, and I have also experienced some of this lighter heart and peaceful spirit you testified to. Although I still struggle with fear and long for freedom from all the things that hinder me, my intuition tells me that I may need to do some more forgiving in the future.

Thank you for writing and publishing your testimony. It has opened a door in my life that God has walked through, that's good. I have longed for a book that speaks honestly of the hard travel on the road to recovery from trauma, I feel Christians here [Britain] need more of these honest accounts ...

In late 2003, while I was touring North America and the UK, many people – especially those in Northern Ireland, who seemed able to identify and empathize with my suffering – echoed similar sentiments. However, I found that people in North America were less interested in hearing a message of suffering and forgiveness. Living in such a cosy place, they perhaps do not want to engage with the message of suffering. They seem uninterested in reading such a painful book. But I thank God for directing me to many good people around the world whose words of encouragement have motivated me to write. Without them, this book would have been forever sleeping in deep, silent therapy.

It has not been an easy ride to write this book. When I first returned to Cambodia to teach and lecture at the Phnom Penh Bible School, I went to visit my home town and a few of my surviving relatives. I thought a great deal about this trip and looked forward to renewing my links with my family members. When I reached their home I greeted them with deep affection and was so pleased to see them. I told them about my new-found faith and all it had meant to me, but to my horror, they reacted angrily. One of my cousins said, 'You have been to university in a Western country, and after such a luxury you should at least have brought us money and food; instead you bring this Jesus. We need money, not Jesus.' I felt totally rejected by them and it hurt me deeply. Tears began to form, but I steeled myself from letting them see my emotion and chose to love them, whatever they said to me. During the time I was at the Phnom Penh Bible School I took the long journey frequently to see them, to try to build some relationship with them. This was actually a hazardous journey as I went by boat on the Tonle Sap River, and often these boats were shot at from the riverbanks by Khmers who wanted easy cash. If I went by road, there were robbers and bandits who would hold travellers to ransom if they thought they would be easy prey for cash, in a society that lived in dire poverty.

I kept sharing the message of hope and faith in our

Lord Jesus with my relatives and particularly with my surviving sister, Sopheap. I prayed for them all, and about six months later, my sister's family committed their lives to Jesus. I was overjoyed, and every other week I made the journey to her house to pray with them and to teach them more about Jesus. I continued this for another six months, and then felt led to start church planting in the area where I had been brought up. God richly blessed me during this period and I met and married Phaly, my wife. When Phaly was expecting our first child I returned to Canada temporarily so that she could have the baby in a good, Western-style hospital.

When we returned with our son Philos we were all so happy, but in my position as a teacher and counsellor at Phnom Penh Bible School, I began to realize the extent of the 'fall-out' from the Killing Fields era. Thousands, particularly in my age group, were desperately trying to cope with the traumas they had been through during that period. I made a decision to resign from the Bible School, as I had such a burden from the Lord to start planting churches in my home area. Beginning with my sister's family, I had a vision to widen out and even cover the countryside where my family was buried. At the same time I met Pastor Pak Soon Lau, an OMF missionary from Singapore. He too shared a deep conviction about church planting in my area. We took a trip together to visit the villages around my home town. We met together for a period of six months to pray about this, and he felt strongly that the Lord had sent me to take on this responsibility.

After Philos had been born in Canada, we struggled to find the finance to return to Cambodia, but I reasoned that since God had saved my life and had allowed me to find a place of freedom in Canada to study, we could now trust him for this money. Within a few days some kind friends had donated all we needed, so we returned to our land of tears with a fresh determination to help our fellow countrymen who were struggling to come to terms with their loss and tragedies. I had met Pastor Narath at the Bible School, and we found we had a lot in common, so together with Pastor Pak Soon Lau, we established Pastor Narath as the leader in the Pouk area, which was my home territory. I continued to mentor Pastor Narath and helped him to set up a chicken farm to pay his expenses. Our people are still too poor to tithe. Within two years there were three small house churches, and by 2005 two more were added to this group. We planted churches, but we also wanted to make sure the local people had clean drinking water, so we helped to dig over twenty wells.

It was a time when we received much blessing from the Lord and daily gave thanks for his goodness, but nothing had prepared me for the shock that came while I was writing Chapter 3 of this book, 'Living with Anger and Denial'. I was sitting at the computer when the telephone rang. Picking up the receiver, I heard the voice of my much-loved only surviving sister: 'My husband, Chhunly Hourt, has been robbed of his motorbike and left dead on the roadside.' This tragic news shocked me deeply, and I felt as though my heart had been cut through. I hung up the phone and took my wife in my arms, telling her that robbers had killed Chhunly. The shock paralysed us both, but I soon had to take action, and rushed off to collect his body from the murder scene. I reflected upon the fact that he had been my only surviving immediate male family member, and although

I had faced many storms in my life, this was like being hit by a tornado. It took time for the awful truth to sink in, and I was overwhelmed by anger when I returned home in the middle of the night and could not sleep at all. I continually tried to figure out what was wrong with my family, and I asked God why this had happened to me again. I felt torn apart by the tragic death of my brother-in-law and could not think about writing on forgiveness. After the funeral, my two angry nephews challenged me with a giant question: 'Uncle, would you forgive the killers if the police caught them?' They knew that earlier in the year, I had been to see my family's killers and had forgiven them. Now, I did not know how to respond. It took me several months to overcome my anger; only then was I able to complete this book.

I have nothing to offer you in the way of a formula or theory on forgiveness. I can only speak from my own experiences. I would like to ask you not to let the hurt inside your heart turn to bitterness and take root. It will ruin your life in many different ways, robbing you of the joy of life. You will reap a harvest of bitterness and miserable depression. The power of forgiveness from the Lord Jesus Christ has set me free from the bondage of bitterness, and I sincerely hope this book will help you to follow him.

Before making the decision to see the killers of my family, I asked several people for their advice. Unbelieving Cambodians told me that it would open up the grave again and that I should leave alone the things that had been buried. 'Do not wake up a ghost. Let it sleep in peace,' they said. I understood well that Cambodian people have learned to live in silence. I knew that opening up the wound would create fresh pain, but suppressing it would not heal anything. Finally, I decided to make the trip, but before going I emailed many friends to ask for their prayer support:

> I would like to ask you to pray for me in this forthcoming trip to meet my family's killers. I will travel to Kokpreach village, in the northern part of Siemreap province to meet them and to take the message of forgiveness. I have decided to cancel my right to take revenge. I think it will be hard for me to face them but I am willing to experience hurt and pain again. It will be very emotional for me but I thank God for granting me the courage to face this unwanted emotional legacy. Cambodian people love to say, 'After the rain, the sky will become clear again.' After I meet them, my heart will be free from the bondage of doubt. Please pray for me. In His mission,
> Reaksa.

I received a number of emails from friends who encouraged me to go with the strength of the Lord. They wrote such things as:

> Give them the Scriptures and show them from the example of Jesus to those that killed Him, 'Forgive them, for they know not what they do'. Read that story to them, underline it and give them the Scriptures as a gift. That is the only reason you are there and able to do what the Lord has asked you to do. This will be the only way they will be able to see the love of God through you.

> I am amazed at the work of God's grace in your life. I remember well the many conversations you and I have had about your life. To think that now you are on a mission of forgiveness is proof of the greatness of God and the love of Jesus in your life. We will pray for you over the next few

days as you make this very difficult journey. May God give you strength, and peace, and may He keep the powers of evil away from you.

Reaksa, I would never see myself in your shoes. When I read your prayer request, I would never imagine how you would deal with the family's killers when you face them. I am very proud of you. You polish your life by following the Lord's example. I pray that the Lord will be with you throughout your journey to meet your family's killers. Be strong. 'I can do everything through Him who gives me strength' (Philippians 4:13).

I have an ornate, yet simple cross that my brother gave me for Christmas one year that sits on the shelf but has great meaning. The greatest gift is for forgiveness – the cross would remind them. You may go one step further and offer to help them start a chicken farm. I would be willing to assist financially in that endeavour if it is practical and prudent. My family and I will pay for you. Thank you for your willingness to present the risen Christ in that way.

Revenge will be taken care of by God. You can rest in that thought. It is not your duty at all. You are a far better man than the killers if your heart is big enough to forgive. Do not have any expectations. Do not be upset if the killers do not seek your forgiveness or listen to you or treat you in the right way. Your duty is only to do what is right, even if they do not do what is right.

I pray that they will see through your example the One whose forgiveness they so desperately need. May their hard hearts be completely broken. May God give you much grace and special emotional strength at this testing time as you seek to magnify and follow Christ.

This is a tremendous lesson in forgiveness to me. I have used your story in many sermons, and I am looking forward to your next book. This will be a spiritual lesson for us. Thank you for being God's messenger to us.

Reaksa, you may just open this before you travel today to meet your family's killers. Here is an encouraging thought about your desire to meet those whom you wish to forgive. You are actually bringing the message of forgiveness to many other hearts. No one can return to them to say they forgive, but you can say it for the many others who have gone forever. There must be a whole lot of Khmer in their late 40s and 50s that need to hear those words of forgiveness from the lips of someone who can speak for the dead. What a load they must be carrying in their memories and hearts. Maybe some of your quiet church leaders or others who filter in or hear you on the street corners are people whose hearts are laden down needing to hear words of forgiveness. God has put you here 'for such a time as this' just the same as He put Esther from the Bible in her place of service; you are there so that you can speak words of forgiveness in a meaningful way to the people of Cambodia – 'Father, forgive them for they didn't know what they were doing'. It's the same prayer and the same heart of the Father and of the Son.

I'm so moved by the real true commission that Jesus gave his disciples the very first time He appeared to them after the resurrection in John 20:21. He said I'm sending you just like the Father sent me. Receive the Holy Spirit and FORGIVE. Go out to a world in need and FORGIVE. Father sent Him on a mission of FORGIVENESS and He commissioned each of us with the same mission of FOR-GIVENESS.

And what a commission! – How frightening! – How serious! – Whoever's sins we forgive, they are forgiven, and whoever's sins we withhold, they are not forgiven. What a mammoth ministry of forgiveness He has commissioned us to live and pass on to others. I have been very moved by this and reminded to pray for many Khmer people in the age group of the 40s and 50s and older. They are the ones truly needing God's 'binding up' and 'healing' (Psalm 147, especially v. 3). I trust these thoughts that are guiding my prayers will be a blessing as you travel.

I had a few friends who had also lost their families during the dark period of the Khmer Rough regime. When they went back to their villages, they killed all those people who had been involved in killing their families. They were trying to pursue honour for their families. Now, I was about to make my trip to meet my family's killers and forgive them. The people in Cambodian society would perceive me as an abnormal person, as different from others. My trip would never make sense to non-believers, or to some believers either, but more importantly, it would make sense for me as a follower of Jesus Christ. I needed to get the unfinished business done without further delay, and to bring the message of forgiveness to my family's killers. Obeying my Lord's commands would bring healing to my wounds.

I had discussed with my wife and my sister the possibility of my making the trip to meet my enemies. My wife was greatly concerned for my safety, but she did not try to stop me going to meet them. She encouraged me to take time to pray and listen to the Lord. My sister was not happy because she could not see that it could do any good. Instead, she thought they should come to meet me and ask for forgiveness, which logically was right. What I intended to do was not normal in Cambodian culture. I may have thought that I was being very strong in going to meet the family's killers, but in fact, I felt very weak and had many apprehensions. It had taken me four years since my return to Cambodia to make this decision, and I knew that such a journey would never make sense to many people, so I felt deeply insecure. I had to learn to trust the Lord and pray for this special trip. Despite my uneasiness, words of encouragement from many good friends had strengthened my soul. In addition, Psalm 23:3-4 helped me to put my trust in the Lord:

> ... he restores my soul.
> He guides me in paths of righteousness
>   for his name's sake.
> Even though I walk
>   through the valley of the shadow of death,
> I will fear no evil,
>   for you are with me;
> your rod and your staff,
>   they comfort me.

As I look back over my life, I can see that the Lord spared my life from the grave for a special purpose. He now wanted me to bring the message of forgiveness through Jesus Christ to my family's killers. He had restored me thus far and would take me further on; all I needed to do was to trust in his security. He would guide me and protect me.

CHAPTER TWO

MARCHED TO A GRAVE

The Unwanted Journey

Before I went to meet the killers, I was reminded of many things. I looked back to those early days when we were a happy family. Darker memories haunted me and could never be erased from my mind. So that you may understand some of the traumas I suffered at the hands of the Khmer Rouge, I invite you to join me on a painful journey through my memories. I had to walk down a long, hard road and make a decision to obey the Lord's teaching to forgive my enemies and find a way of reconciliation. It has not been easy, but finally it has brought me peace of mind and a way forward in serving the Lord by using my experiences to help others.

A few days after 17 April 1975, our family, like many others, was forced to leave our home when the Khmer Rouge came to power. We were taken captive and set to labouring in the countryside. Working hard from dawn to dusk, with very little to eat and nowhere comfortable to spend the night, we became exhausted, demoralized and filled with despair. We lived under a regime of terror where the smallest act of disobedience to the soldiers brought death. After two years of this dreadful existence we were all starving. I watched helplessly as my friends gradually died of starvation. Their relatives were too weak to carry their emaciated corpses to a grave.

One memory I cannot erase was when my younger brother, who was only ten years old, was wrongly accused of stealing some corn. The evil soldiers tied his hands behind his back and beat him mercilessly. They kicked him in the face so many times that he was unrecognizable. As I stood by helplessly, I wanted God to take away my life, because the pain of seeing my brother suffer like this was unbearable. I would rather they had tortured me than him. My parents were also unable to do anything, as even one word from any of us would have meant death. My father was overpowered by speechless anger and my mother was equally distraught. My poor brother was then dragged round the village to show what would happen to anyone else who stole or disobeyed the soldiers' brutal rule in any way.

They repeated the same kind of torture on one of my older brothers, and all of us began to lose any hope of life. Indeed, we all wanted to die. I was enraged by the injustice and angry with God, Buddha and the evil *chlops*. If I'd had a gun I would have killed them immediately. Anger and revenge burned in my heart with an intensity that gave me deep pain. When I went to bed, I could not sleep and I despaired that any of us would ever get out of this horror alive. Why was this happening to my entire family? I cried to God to stop all this evil, but it seemed that he did not hear my cry. My mother prayed to Buddha, but there was no answer. Death seemed inevitable, whether by starvation or by execution at the hands of these evil soldiers.

We felt that no one heard our cry for justice. We were

victims whose every aspect of life was subject to the Khmer Rouge's torture. They could do whatever they wanted; we were their pawns in a deadly game. Their justice system turned on the head of a hoe. For us, true justice was dead. Defenceless, helpless and very weak, we were like chickens in a cage waiting to be slaughtered for food. We were not sure when it would be our turn, and that was the source of our despair. There was nothing we could do but obey their evil laws. We could not run anywhere. In a jail without walls, we were the victims of an evil that had no boundaries. We could not die instantly, but at last we realized that this terrible existence was soon to end.

I went out early one morning to fetch some water, and saw the *chlops* sharpening their knives and axes. I ran back and told my father what I had seen. '*Papa,*' I said, 'I'm afraid they are going to kill us this morning!' My father was shocked to hear this, and he opened his eyes wider than I had ever seen before. It was a sign of shock and despair. He did not speak at all but I could tell that, like me, he had become very desperate. I fed my youngest brother and dressed him, and then a teenage *chlop* came up to our house. Now I knew for sure that something terrible was about to happen to us. He came to see my father and said, '*Mith bong* [comrade brother], the *angkar loeu* [leader] is inviting you to meet him in the shelter now.' My arms and legs shook with fear.

My father responded, 'I will be there in a few minutes. I need to get dressed first.' After he was dressed he came to tell me, 'Reaksa, whatever happens to me today, I want you and your two older brothers who have been sent to work with the youth mobile team to kill these people for me.'

With that, he went off and I trailed behind him to see what the *angkar loeu* would do to him. Right away a *chlop* arrested my father and bound his arms behind his back. One said to my father, 'You are the *khmang* [enemy] of the *angkar loeu.*'

My father asked them, 'What is wrong with me? I have not done anything wrong.'

And then he was kicked in the stomach and they said, 'You are the *khmang* of the *angkar loeu.* You served the American soldiers. We will destroy you today. If we keep you, we gain nothing, but if we kill you, we lose nothing.'

When I heard that cruel pronouncement, I knew right away that they would certainly kill all of us. I ran back to my younger brothers and sister right away and told them, '*Papa* has been arrested. They are going to kill us today. I don't know what to do now!'

I could not stand still and I could not sit still. A great weakness came over me. As they realized that death would come soon, they started to tremble uncontrollably like me. Only Sopheak did not shake. He was sad, but he seemed to have no fear of dying. I could never have imagined that the fear of death could be so terrible. I hugged my younger brothers and sister but my weak hands could not hold onto them. They knew that I was terribly frightened and I could tell that they felt the same.

Then a *chlop* dragged my father back to the house and the others called us to come outside. They bound my hands behind my back but did not tie my younger brothers and sister. When they realized there was no one to carry my youngest brother, they unbound me so that I could carry him. Then they told us, 'We will send you to school, because you are the *khmang* of the *angkar loeu.* Go with your father now!' They put us in an ox-cart and drove us from the village. We followed the Khmer Rouge soldiers who dragged my father along so that we had to watch his humiliation.

When we got into the jungle, there were other 'new liberated' children with their fathers, some of whom we knew. I did not see their mothers nor did I see my mother. She and my older sister were probably still reaping in the field where they had gone early in the morning. I looked at the other children and could tell that they were frightened like me. I held onto my youngest brother but my arms would not stop trembling, and it was very hard to sit on the ox-cart with him because I felt so weak.

Even then, I wanted to hit the *chlop* who was driving the cart, but I did not have anything to hit him with. Besides, what would I do with my brother then? If I hit the *chlop*, I would not be able to kill him, though I might hurt him. When I thought further about my younger brothers and sister who were with me, I decided to give up and wait patiently to be executed. The cart took us about three kilometres from the village. One *chlop* came to stop the cart a short distance away, because they had not yet finished digging the grave. We waited there for a while. I got off the cart and carried my youngest brother to my father, who knelt to kiss him. After he had kissed his youngest son, he kissed the rest of the children. I gave him a hug but he could not hug me in return because his arms were bound. He could not say anything either. Instead I said, 'Papa, I would like to thank you so much for being my father.' It was so painful to speak even those few words. I wanted to say more to him, but I could not. Feelings choked the words in my throat.

Faintly I heard my father say, 'Reaksa, my heart is

being torn to pieces. I have lived long enough, but you, your brothers and your sisters are too young to die. They are so innocent. Look, look at your youngest brother; he does not know anything yet. He does not know that we are going to be killed soon. He is smiling and laughing. Does everybody else know that we are going to be killed?'

'Yes, I told them after I saw the *chlops* arrest you in the meeting shelter.'

My youngest sister cried, 'Papa, I want to see *Mak*, I want to hug her, I want to give her a kiss and say good-bye to her. Where is she?'

My sister's words choked my father, I could tell. He did not know how to answer her. I felt the same as my father and was almost speechless. Oh God! How could this happen to my family? I hugged my sister, holding her tightly in my arms and trying to encourage her by saying, '*Mak* will come soon.' That was all I could say.

Five *chlops* were looking at us and laughing, and I wished that I had a gun to kill them right away. Hurt and anger welled up in my soul. In contrast, Sopheak was calm and brave. He was not afraid of being killed for he had already tasted death. He seemed to know that after he was dead, he would not feel pain any more. His arms and legs were not shaking like mine.

The other families were saying their farewells to one another. Were they as afraid as we were? I turned my attention from them, for I just wanted to spend time with my family and talk to them before we died. My younger sister screamed to my father for help, '*Papa*, please help me! I am scared, *PAPA!*' My father did not answer her. He was a helpless man who was about to be killed. I could not imagine what he was thinking or feeling, but I sensed that his heart was wrung with agony.

My father was now in front of the two wells that they had enlarged to be our graves. There were the *chlops*, wearing black uniforms and handmade red Cambodian neck-scarves, waiting for us to arrive. They kicked my father's legs, forcing him to kneel. He turned his head to look at me, and I saw them hack at his head with a hoe, and then he fell into the grave with a terrible scream. I screamed too: 'Where are you, God? Help us!' Screaming was useless.

Then one of the evil *chlops* jumped into the grave to finish off my father. I did not want to look at all, but I could not close my eyes; they saw every single act that was done to my father. The horrific scene before me filled my heart with a fire of rage that was intensified because I could do nothing to help him or the others. I thought I would die of suffocation before they hit me.

Then it was our turn. They called us to kneel in front of the grave, and as I knelt down, a man called Mao hit me from behind and I fell into the grave on top of my father, who was not yet dead! I heard his last few breaths. Then there was nothing. My younger brothers, my sister and others tumbled into the grave too, landing on top of me. Finally, they clubbed my baby brother. The first three times they struck him, he screamed loudly; then they clubbed him once more and I didn't hear him again. I was still conscious but I could not move. I knew that my siblings and the other children were not yet dead, for the *chlops* jumped into the grave to hack wildly at us. In their frenzy, they mangled everybody with their axes, but they missed me. After they had finished their slashing spree, they climbed up out of the grave. I heard one of them say, 'I think that one is not yet dead.' At whom was he pointing? I could not see because I was lying face down on my father's body, covered by the bodies of my brothers and others, but I found out very quickly. One *chlop* jumped down into the grave again to pull somebody off me, and then he hit me with the hoe once more, but not hard enough to end my life. They thought that I was truly dead and did not slash at me as they had done to the others. If I had moved my legs or hands then, they would have finished me off. I could not move because of the weight of dead bodies lying on top of me.

They began to fill the grave, but I heard someone say, 'Don't bury them now, because there are some more *khmangs* to be destroyed.' Assuming that everybody was already dead, they left the grave open and went off to find other victims to feed to the earth.

I had only one sensation then. I could taste death as blood flowed out through my nose and mouth, nearly choking me. I wanted to get out of there but could not move. Pain and panic took hold and I had to force myself to calm down. They would not fill in the grave right away and, if they left the grave soon, I might be able to get away.

Five minutes after they had gone I tried to disentangle myself from the dead bodies. It took me almost half an hour to move out from under them because I was so weak. After I had climbed out, I turned around to look at the bodies. Everyone was lying dead with their throats slashed. My two younger brothers' brains had spilled out. As for my father, his throat was slashed and split wide open. His eyes were open as though he were looking at me. He was already dead but his eyes were not closed, so I stretched down and put my right hand on his face and closed them.

After I had checked on everybody in the family, I sank

down in despair, lying on top of those horribly mutilated bodies, waiting to be executed too. As I waited, I cried and cried until I had no more tears. I cried to God to hear me and also to Buddha. I cried until I lost consciousness. When I awakened, I knew that I did not want to run anywhere. I still remembered how my father had encouraged us to live together and to die together. I wanted them to come back and finish the job by executing me, because my head was almost exploding with grief and emptiness. Young though I was, at that moment I realized that my life was meaningless. I felt as though I was swimming in a sea without sight of land. My only desire was to let them kill me; the pain was too much to bear and I didn't want to live like this for the rest of my life.

I waited there for about an hour, but nobody came. Once more I climbed out of the grave and looked down at my family members lying dead in a pool of blood. I walked for a few metres, but then I saw *chlops* appearing from the west and south, dragging other people towards the open grave. If I had waited at the grave for a few more minutes, the *chlops* would have captured me once again. Quickly I looked for a hiding place in the woods. I wanted to see who else they would kill. Suddenly, I saw my beloved mother and older sister stumbling towards the grave. Their faces were covered with *kramas* (Cambodian scarves) and they were crying bitterly. My mouth opened to yell so that my mother would turn round and I could see her face once more. If I yelled, maybe I could get their attention, so they would come and kill me instead of my mother. No sound came and I felt strangely paralysed. I tried again, but it was as though a power was upon me and behind me, preventing me from crying out loud.

They clubbed my mother and older sister, and I saw them fall into the grave too. All I wished for at that moment was to tell my mother how much I loved her. I wished we had been able to say goodbye. At the same time, my heart burned with rage, and I wanted to kill all these murderers right away in order to save my mother and sister, but I was powerless and totally helpless. I couldn't even scream at them to come and kill me. I watched as the *chlops* carelessly closed the grave and then left.

When the sun had almost set I crept out to the grave and pounded on it with my hands and hit it with my head. '*Mak*, please take me with you, take me with you! I don't want to live!' I called to my mother but she did not hear me. So finally, I bowed before the grave and made three promises to my family. 'Mother, father, brothers and sisters, as long as I live, I will avenge your deaths. If not, I will become a monk, and if I cannot fulfil these two promises I won't live in Cambodia any more.'

After I had made these promises, I realized I could not stay there. I began to think about what I needed to do to survive. Survival seemed impossible in the jungle, especially since there was no water to drink. I sat down and cried and cried and just wanted to die. Thirst and hunger overcame me, because I had not had anything to drink or eat since my younger brother and I returned from fishing in the early morning. It was getting dark and I had never been in the jungle alone. I was afraid of wild animals that could easily eat me alive. I knew that if I slept on the ground close to the grave, the animals would kill me and eat me, because they could smell the blood of the victims. I knew that I had to move away from the grave to find a place to sleep for the night.

About half a mile away I climbed a tree to get some rest. I will never forget the horror of that first night alone in the jungle as an inky darkness came down on everything. I heard something run along on the ground but couldn't see what it was. As I despaired in this darkness, how I wished the sun would rise early and lighten this place of death! Mosquitoes bit me badly, so I tried to keep moving all the time, but I was tired out and weak through lack of water and food. My neck was badly swollen from the blows I had received from the soldiers and I couldn't breathe properly; it was as though something was blocked in my chest. Every time I moved, pain shot through my chest and neck. I thought, 'This is because of my terrible *karma*', and I wondered about throwing myself from the tree so that I would die in peace and not suffer. But what if the fall did not kill me? I would then suffer even more, so I ended up hugging the tree-trunk the whole night through.

I drank some dew in the early morning but it was not enough to quench my thirst. I was also hungry, so I returned to the jungle to search for food. After an hour, I found some bamboo shoots and broke them off for my lunch. They tasted disgusting but I had nothing else. I was lucky to get them, because it was hard to find edible food in an unfamiliar place, and I was unwilling to go deeper into the jungle, as I feared getting lost.

After eating the shoots, I returned to the grave. I didn't want to be there, but something drew me back. The spot filled me with horror, but I had nowhere else to go and was reluctant to leave the bodies of my dear family. I spent three more nights in the forest, but then realized that if I was to survive, I must find someone somewhere.

I began coughing, and blood came out of my mouth

and nose. Every time I coughed I felt a deep pain in my chest. I realized that I wouldn't live much longer if I continued to stay in the jungle. The intensity of the pain drove me to go to the village and ask the *chlops* to end my life. I walked about three kilometres in that direction and came to a small watermelon farm tended by two elderly *tatas*. I sat outside for a few hours, unsure whether I wanted to be seen by them. They didn't know me but I knew them because they were from the village where I used to live.

Around four o'clock, I knew that the *tatas* were about to return to the village, so I decided to approach them. One of them looked at me in amazement and said, 'Chao, where are you from?'

I pointed eastwards. 'I came from the village there. Could I have some water to drink?'

After I had drunk the water, one of the men said, 'You must be lost.'

I replied, 'No, I was just passing by and I became thirsty and thought of asking you for water.'

They did not recognize me so I sat there for a while with them, struggling to decide how much I should let them know. Finally I decided to tell them the truth. When I told them my story, my name, my father's name and that I belonged to the people who had been killed three days earlier, they did not believe me at all and said that I was lying. They ordered me to leave their shelter because they were about to go home and didn't want to waste their time with me.

I told them that I would leave, but asked them to let me finish my story. I said to one of them, 'Ta, I know your son very well. His name is Bo. He used to take care of the cows and water-buffaloes with me.' He seemed to believe at last and his eyes opened wide, but he didn't think I was a real human being – only a ghost. He was frightened and tried to cast a spell to make me disappear. I told him, 'Stop trying to cast a spell; it won't work with me, because I'm not a ghost!'

The other man tried to do the same, but it didn't work and their foreheads got sweaty. They were about to give up and run away when I told them, 'Look at my hands, my body. Touch me.' They did just that and said, 'He's not a ghost. He really is Reaksa!' Then they asked, 'How did you get out of the grave? Didn't they kill you?'

I told them the whole story but it took a while to convince them. However, once they believed me they encouraged me not to go back to the village, as they were sure I would be killed. They advised me to run as far as I could, but I had nowhere to go. They began to feel sorry for me, but they were also afraid of getting into trouble with the *angkar loeu* if they aided a *khmang*.

So all I said was, '*Tatas*, tell the people in the village that I am still alive. Let the *chlops* finish me, but I want some rice to eat before they kill me. I will be waiting around this place.' Then I left the watermelon farm and they watched me until I disappeared into the jungle.

I looked for a place to sleep that was on the ground, because I thought there would be no wild animals in that area, as people talked about a bad spirit in that place, especially in the big tree near by. Some had seen a big ball of fire flying about and it was thought that if a person were to see that ball of fire, he would get sick and die when he arrived home. So everyone was scared of the area, but I was so exhausted that I lay down by the big tree. Before I slept, I said, 'O owner of this place, I would like your permission to sleep here for a night. I hope you don't mind.' Then I fell asleep, but in my dreams I saw some horrible apparitions. It was my third night in the jungle alone, and I knew that I could not stay another night.

In the morning, I went back to the watermelon farm. I expected that the *tatas* would tell my story to the people in the village, and then the evil *chlops* would surely come to finish me off. Tired out, I rested in the shade of a bamboo bush that grew very close to the pathway. An hour later, the four *chlops* who had killed my family came walking towards me carrying axes, hoes and big knives. I knew that they had come to end my life but I was not afraid of them. I could see no future, so death would be just a release from suffering. They stopped by the bamboo bush but they did not see me even though they were standing not very far away. Then they looked directly at me but they still did not see me. Were they blind? I tried to speak but wasn't able to move because it felt as if some great load was on me, holding me down on the ground. Five minutes passed before I could move, then I got up and was not really sure why that had happened. I got out of the bush, came back and lay down on the same spot again, but I didn't experience the same thing. I could move and speak, and I was filled with wonder. It was a miracle, but I could not understand why this had happened.

I left the bush and went back to the watermelon farm where the two *tatas* were waiting for me, and they seemed glad to see me. They told me I was very lucky to be alive, but inside me I had no hope of ever finding a life of happiness again. I had lost so much and seen such terrible things. The past haunted me, the future held no hope and my only reason for living was to avenge the killers of my family. Death would mean freedom from pain, whereas life was meaningless. I had not forgotten the three promises that I had made, but neither did I expect to survive the Killing Fields. The *chlops* liked to say, 'If we keep you we gain nothing, but if we kill you we lose nothing.' There was no reason for them to keep me alive, and yet there were many reasons for them to kill me, and to do so would not be difficult at all.

The *tatas* gave me some food and asked where I had stayed for the night. I pointed to the big tree near by. They were shocked and their eyes opened wide. 'Are you lying, *chao*? You know that no one dares to stay below that tree in the night.' The other blurted out, '*Chao*, did you see anything last night?' I told them about some of the terrifying apparitions that had gone through my tormented mind. They seemed to believe me, then warned me that people who ran away after seeing these ghosts became sick when they got home, and their hair dropped out before they suddenly died. But it was not an evil spirit that I saw clubbing me from behind with a hoe. It was *chlops*, not evil spirits, who had killed my family and the other people, and I was more afraid of these evil men than I was of any evil spirit.

The sun was about to set and the two *tatas* were going home. I was not really sure what would happen to me and I was in a poor condition. I had had more than enough pain, so I marched back to the village to be executed by the *chlops*. On the way back, I talked with the two *tatas*, pretending that I feared nothing. In fact, inside, I was riddled with anxiety and tension and often felt quite sick. The *tatas* wished me good luck. As I approached the village it was getting dark, but to my utter astonishment all the people in the village were waiting for me! They welcomed me, cried with me and moaned with me; they touched me, hugged me and spoke consoling words. What a contrast to the way they had behaved before, when they had accused me of being a *khmang*! This time they called me 'a special one' and 'the resurrected one' and 'the only lucky one', and tied white threads onto my left hand and invited my soul and spirit to come back into me. I could not understand the ritual practice but I just sat down and cried. They took my shirt off and gave me a new one and then gave me some food to eat.

They called a special meeting and all agreed that I could live when a man in the village named Mov said he would take me into his home and become my foster father. I had promised to kill the *chlops* one day, and now there was a man who was blocking me from doing it. Vengeance was a sign of honour for me. Now, instead of being relieved and thankful I was filled with confusion. How long would this last? Could I trust their word?

After the meeting was over, Mov took me to his house and accepted me as his foster son. At first it was very hard for me to call him *pook* – father – because he was not my father. My only father had just been killed, but somehow I would have to learn to respect this new man as my foster father because he was prepared to accept me. He admitted, 'I do not know why I stood up to defend you. It felt as though there was someone telling me to save your life. Since I have done it, you are now my son.' I knelt down and thanked him for saving me.

In the morning, *pook* Mov went out to find some traditional herbal medicine, because I had told him of the pain in my chest and the bleeding from my nose. The medicine was bitter and difficult to swallow, but after a few days I could breathe more easily and the pain in my chest was gone. If only my emotional pain could have been healed so quickly!

By early 1979 the Khmer Rouge regime had been driven out by the Vietnamese army. I went back to the city to live with my only surviving sister, Sopheap Himm, and later I went to my aunt's family in Siemreap. I went back to school and started a new life. In 1983, I joined the police force with one burning desire – to use this position to avenge the deaths of my beloved family. I had survived, but my heart was full of anger, bitterness and an overwhelming passion to keep the promises I had made to my dead family. As a policeman, I carried a gun, so I had the power to kill my enemies. But I could not do it, and when I had an opportunity with one of my brother's murderers, some strange force came upon me, and although I had my finger on the trigger of the gun, I was unable to press it. Life was unbearably miserable when I found that I could not fulfil my promises. In mid 1984, I escaped to a Thai refugee camp, but I experienced more horrors on the journey.

I was arrested by Khmer Resistance soldiers who were fighting against the Vietnamese army in Cambodia. They accused me of being a spy, and when that accusation failed, they said I was bringing poisons into their camp. I was subjected to a shameful body search and they found nothing, but four others who were with me had some cruel things done to them. One of them was escaping with his wife, and a soldier raped her in front of us. People who escaped from Cambodia often had gold on them, so they were using this ruse as an excuse to steal any gold we had. Conditions in the first camp were simply terrible, and I was forced to leave, as they only gave food to women and children. The journey to Khao I Dang camp was equally hazardous, but I found it at last, and when I was questioned about the route I had taken, the officers said it was a miracle that I had ever arrived at all.

It was November 1984 when at last I began to work in this camp and had food and shelter, but a great restlessness came upon me and I fell into a deep depression. The camp was vast and housed 120,000 refugees, among whom were some caring Christians who daily spread the message of Christ's love and forgiveness and promised a new life of faith in him. Buddhism hadn't helped me, so what good would any other religion do? My cries for help to God and Buddha had gone unheard and certainly unanswered, so I kept myself to myself and lived daily with utter misery, despair and hopelessness. When I slept fitfully at night I had terrible nightmares about the grave and all the unspeakable things I had seen and witnessed. I thought the only way forward was for me to go as far away from Cambodia as I could and begin a new life, perhaps as a Buddhist priest. I went to the camp's Immigration and Naturalization Service so that I could go to America. They helped me to fill in the forms, and I waited for the application to be accepted. Finally I was told that it had been rejected. This drove me into a deeper pit of despair. Then, at long last, I admitted that I needed help from God.

I joined the Christian meetings in the camp and listened to their prayers. There was a peace within this group that I had never experienced elsewhere. I was impressed by the way they sang their songs, but when I asked questions about suffering, they didn't seem to have the right answers. I wrote to a cousin who was living in the United States to see if he could send me some money. He wrote back telling me about Jesus, to my astonishment. I resented his letter but I began to ask myself, 'Who is this Jesus?' I told God that I had been through so many traumas and had struggled with such terrible despair and hopelessness that, if he really loved me, he would have to take up my case and deliver me from all these awful pressures. I decided to apply for permission to live in Canada, and I actually told the Lord that if this succeeded, I would then totally trust him. My application was accepted, so I saw this as a sign that God had heard my cries. After my acceptance had been finalized, I began to feel there was at last some hope of a better future for me in Canada.

I arrived in Canada in 1989 and was taken to a reception centre run by World Vision. Back in the camp I had been told what to expect, but just looking at the tall buildings and the fast roads, I found it way past all my expectations and felt bewildered. How could I survive in this concrete jungle? What I had heard and what I had to learn were beyond my imagination. There were times in my new-found freedom when my thoughts went back to my peaceful days in Cambodia: the gentle open countryside with vibrant green rice paddies gleaming in the hot sunshine; the yoked oxen ploughing the fields; the swampy areas filled with water lilies and lotus flowers; the beautiful sugar-palms with their green fronds waving in the breeze. But then memories of the dark times took over, and I was thankful that I was thousands of miles away from all the horrors.

At the World Vision centre that was helping refugees there were so many people who befriended me. This was like a taste of heaven, as these Christians took me to their hearts. They didn't blame my *karma* for all the dreadful things that had happened to me; instead they showed me Christ's great love, a love that had taken him to a cruel death on a cross to pay the price for my sins. He was the sinless Lamb of God who takes away the sins of the world. This was all new to me and so wonderful that it touched my bruised and broken heart and helped to restore me. I made friends with one of the World Vision staff called Chuck Ferguson, and he gave me a Bible to take to my room to read. He prayed with me and made me feel that after all there was a new life for me, and never again would I be alone, for Jesus himself would walk with me.

A year later, I went to Tyndale University College for my bachelor's degree and later to Providence Theological Seminary for my master's degree. I graduated in 1996 and then started a cleaning company. It did well and I had a good income and settled down to my new life in Canada. When I was feeling content, several people asked me if I had considered going back to Cambodia. I told them quite emphatically, 'No, never! Why should I want to return to a place with so many miserable memories?'

Then I received a letter from Dr Duc Nguyen who was working with World Vision USA. He had visited the Phnom Penh Bible School. He told me that the church in Cambodia was growing, that there was a great need for good Christian teaching, and also that many Cambodians needed counselling to overcome their problems. In conclusion, he said I was the most qualified person to do all these things. Would I seriously consider going back to the land where I had been hurt?

CHAPTER THREE

LIVING WITH
ANGER AND DENIAL

Revenge is a sign of honour
for my family

It was a major decision for me to make when I felt the Lord was asking me to return to my homeland. I wondered how I would cope with seeing those places from my childhood and the family grave. But this time I had Jesus with me, so I took the step to return, with his help and support. I have been back in Cambodia three years, teaching at the Phnom Penh Bible School. I now live in my home town and I am planting churches.

Looking back over the last twenty-seven years of my life has brought back many painful memories and the unwanted emotional legacy of all the devastating events that took my family away from me forever. These can never be erased from my mind, but despite the hardships I have been through, I can now see the purpose of my life. God, in his great love for me, understands my pain, and I believe he has brought me to the place where I needed to learn to forgive my family's killers. Writing this chapter caused me deep pain again as I thought of all the injustices and the killers' brutality. Would it be possible for me to forgive and be reconciled to such evil criminals? Does forgiving mean forgetting? How can I ever forget my family? Does forgiving depend on how I feel? How can I summon the emotional energy to face the task of forgiving? Is forgiveness as easy as some people make it sound? These were questions that I often faced during the time when I reviewed my past, and I went through some severe emotional storms.

During the years of the Khmer Rouge and the awful events of my family's deaths, I was too young to fully understand these events in my life. The hurt was so deep that I did not even know how to describe my pain or cope with my negative emotions. The fire of anger in my heart was uncontrollable and my mind was wrongly programmed with a vengeance mentality. The pursuit of vengeance became my ultimate goal in life. I was absolutely determined to seek revenge. This anger and the fire of rage which smouldered unchecked in my heart would ultimately cripple me emotionally. Although I had become a Christian, there were so many things in my life that needed further healing from the Lord. But I couldn't bring myself to tell anyone about these feelings, or I would feel ashamed, so I kept them all bottled up tightly within me.

I continually remembered the three promises I had made at the grave – so much so that revenge became my first priority. Vengeance was the strong will that kept me moving and it was a sign of family honour for me. With such perceptions in my head, I learned to embrace the anger and bitterness inside my heart and wouldn't let them go. In fact, I did not know how to let go. I just wanted to kill the *chlops*. They deserved to be hacked to pieces – by me. The verdict upon them should be death. The power of anger completely took over my life and created only bitterness, hurt, disappointment, hatred and resentment in my soul day after day. I could hardly go about daily life without being overwhelmed by anger and bitterness. Sometimes, I dreamed I was so angry with the killers that I could control it no longer and I killed them all. I felt so happy that I was able to accomplish my promise. This was just a dream, but the reality was that this obsession controlled my thoughts.

I was scared by my anger and I didn't know what to do about it; I was afraid it would erupt in my heart like a volcano. And if it did erupt, what could I do? Inside my heart was a giant ball of fire that I could not control and which kept flaring up. In relationships with the people around me, I found myself being an angry man. Inside my heart, the peace I had known when I had first encountered Jesus had long since disappeared. Everything was restless, chaotic and confused, so that I was unable to handle my anger in a healthy way. I had experienced only the negative manifestations of anger and had never seen anger expressed in healthy, non-destructive ways. So I learned to suppress it. In my culture, expressing anger is not considered appropriate behaviour. I felt deeply pressured by trying to keep my anger under control and often felt that it might explode at any moment. Keeping such unresolved anger inside without being willing to look at it created so much tension and confusion that it was hard for me to move on. I was trapped by my negative emotions.

Over many years, I learned that my anger was associated with the power of vengeance. I wanted to punish those who had killed my family. My justification for this punishment was to inflict suffering on them and ask them how they would have felt in my situation. My standard of justice was to demand their lives in exchange for those of my family. I could not forget or erase the traumatic memories of how they had tied my younger brother's arms behind his back and hung him on a fence, torturing him until he lost consciousness. We were forced to watch what they were doing to him. We could not make any complaint against them. This crushed us psychologically. My older brother was falsely accused as a thief and his arms were tied backwards to a post so that mosquitoes could torment him throughout the night. When these images of torture filled my mind, I burned with the fire of rage. I could not make myself stand still. I was fully occupied by the fire of anger, and the will to avenge took control of my life. All I wanted to do was to settle the score with those people. Sometimes, I fantasized about torturing them the way they had tortured my brothers. I wanted to kick them just as they had kicked my younger brother and hit them the way they had hit my older brother. I wanted them to be bitten by mosquitoes for the whole night so that I could ask them how they felt about the injustice done to them. The pursuit of vengeance was born out of my anger, but the fantasy was not real, although I felt it helped me, just temporarily, to overcome my anger. It helped me to have a sense that I could do something for my family. It helped me to have a moment of accomplishment or a feeling of victory over my enemies, and this, again temporarily, helped to calm my anger.

How could I forget what those cruel soldiers had done to my family? With images of their sufferings still foremost in my mind, I tasted only anger and bitterness in life. I longed only to make those killers suffer as they had made all of us suffer. The strength of my longing to fulfil my promise never subsided. But even if I could kill them, I would never feel satisfied. No matter how just this may have been, it would never replace what had been lost. In my heart, I knew that even if I could kill the whole village, it would never bring a sense of satisfaction. The pain was too great and the anger too deep.

I remembered when I joined the police force, looking for an opportunity to return to the village and turn it into one big grave. I was able to persuade three policemen and five government soldiers to go with me to sweep the whole village. They agreed to help me, but before we made our trip, I hired a man to spy on the village for me. When he came back, he told me that hundreds of Khmer Rouge soldiers were based there, and there was no way I could go to the village with just a few policemen and soldiers. Even though this plan failed, I refused to give up my pursuit of honour on behalf of my family.

I was now back in my own country, and I had embraced Christianity, and yet the emotions of the past still ruled me and wrecked my peace and contentment.

While I was writing this chapter the telephone rang. My only surviving sister, Sopheap, was calling to tell me that her husband had been robbed and killed. The moment I heard this tragic news, I felt as though my heart had been cut in two. I was terribly shocked because her husband and I had been great friends and he had been part of the family. How could God allow another tragedy into my life? Hadn't I had enough sorrow and misery? Immediately the anger began to boil in my heart again and I didn't know what to do with it. I knelt down and cried out to God, 'Why is such a terrible thing happening to me again? Why, oh why, oh why ... ?'

I made a phone call to my church-planting partner pastor, Pak Soon Lau, telling him the sad news. Then I went out into the deep night to pick up my brother-in-law's body and bring it home. I took my two nephews along with me and, as soon as they saw their father's body, rage ignited them too. I was horrified to see the scene where my dear brother-in-law had been killed. It reminded me of my family's deaths all over again.

A few weeks after the funeral, my sister's sons expressed their determination to settle the score on behalf of their father. My older nephew wanted the murderers to be killed. He planned to bribe the local authorities to search for the robbers and kill them. He told his mother that he could not erase from his mind the scene of his father lying dead. He had firmly decided that, even if it took ten years, he would never give up his determination to settle the score. The younger nephew was also in a rage. He wanted to poke the robbers' eyes out and chop them into pieces and pour fish sauce on their bodies. How well I could identify with them, because for many years I had felt just like them! I too had been filled with a strong determination to kill those who had killed my family. So I didn't know what to say to my nephews. I could not blame them because I could identify only too well with them. But I also knew that, eventually, even if it took as long as ten or twenty years, they would have to learn to forgive those robbers. Then I thought to myself, 'Have you forgiven your family's killers?'

However, even a few months after my brother-in-law had been murdered, I couldn't bring myself to write again. I felt weak, motiveless and, worst of all, I found myself burning with internal anger. I was angry at the evil thing that had been done to my brother-in-law. How callous those robbers were, to kill a man just for a cheap motorbike that had cost only a few hundred dollars! All I could see in the tragic death of my brother-in-law was that people who do not know God value life very cheaply.

I didn't realize the extent of the anger that I had been living with for many years – years of longing to take revenge. And what had those years brought me? Only anger, rage, bitterness, and no peace. The anger kept boiling in my heart but I did not know how to tell anyone about it. From the outside I looked so peaceful, but inside I was full of conflict, confusion and insecurity. I found it impossible to move on; in fact I was torn apart by this internal fury. No one could see it and no one could understand my pain or my bitterness. I could not talk to anybody about the hurt and the anguish of my heart because I was so afraid that other people would ask me about what had happened to my family. About five years after I had lost my family, I totally denied everything that had happened. It was too painful to tell anyone about my loss, and I could trust no one. I felt no one would understand my anger and bitterness, so I avoided all kinds of people because I had no courage to tell them about my pain. Rather, I felt that I could live with the painful memories and that I would keep the traumatic events in my life buried in my mind. So, from day to day, I tried to hide my feelings and control my anger, bitterness and hurt. I suppressed all of these negative emotions to the point of numbness.

However, over the years, I learned that such emotional numbness affected every single part of my life. I lost the joy of life and was in a state of desperate despair.

Any hope I might have of moving forward was shrouded in darkness. How could I move on when my life was ruled by anger? Yet I kept on denying what had happened. I was not only afraid that people would ask me what had happened to my family, but I also feared facing my own horrific past experiences. I feared that the pain would be too great for me to bear. In order to handle my pain, I had learned to suppress it, but in doing this over several years, I came to an impasse where I found I was emotionally numb. Living with this numbness necessitated pretending that nothing had happened to me. I was not hurt badly; in fact I was doing great! Nothing bothered me, so I could move on with my life. No need to worry about me! Nevertheless, the deep pain in my heart grew daily during this period of denial.

Actually, I became particularly good at blocking out my past painful experiences. I remember one occasion when a friend of my brother asked me, 'Are you Reaksa, the one who survived the mass execution and escaped from the grave?' It was a perfectly valid question but it hit me like a bomb. However, because I was so good at denial, I answered, 'I am not Reaksa. You've got the wrong person. Nothing has happened to me.' Then I walked away from him, and in doing that I also walked away from reality. By denying the truth and pretending that nothing had happened to me, I deceived myself. It might be fun to fool someone else, but fooling myself was very painful. In a strange way, I protected myself from facing the truth, but it created in me a deep distrust of everyone.

Now I had to deal with another kind of hurt: the guilt of denial ate me alive. Even though I was good at it, denial was very difficult to live with. The truth hurt enough, but denying it was even more destructive. Denial would never set me free from the bondage of guilt. The psychological impact of living in denial was long lasting, infecting my life for many years. I did not know how to accept my hurt and pain. Running away from it was no good, but I could not bring myself to accept it. Wherever I went, I carried a kind of psychological red-alert warning with me that meant I tried to avoid all kinds of people, especially those who had known my family. I did not have the courage to face them asking me questions about what had happened. I was afraid that speaking about it would cause pain, and I just could not bear any more hurt. In addition to avoiding interaction with strangers, I constantly attempted to isolate myself from people who knew me. Even though I had to hang around with them, I did not like to. I was forced to set an alarm in my head whereby, if they asked me about my family, I would have to walk away from them because I could not handle my past trauma.

On occasions when I could not avoid these question-ers, I just admitted that my family had been killed but said that it did not affect me; I could live with it because I was a strong man and could handle pain. Actually, I was living with two faces – the real face with the painful heart, and the fake face of self-denial. Wearing two faces created so much confusion in my life that at times I wasn't sure who was the real me. It was hard to accept the pain but it was painful to deny the truth. How could I say that it did not affect me when I was so sad and the anger kept boiling over in my soul? Eventually, I fell into such a spiral of pain that there seemed no way out.

Sometimes, I just acknowledged that I was hurt, but I believed that I did not have to deal with my pain because it was my *karma*. I deserved such a bad *karma* and reminded myself that other people who had lost their relatives and family were in more pain than I was. When I could not completely block out the pain, I used to tell myself that others had similar problems and that perhaps mine were no worse than theirs. During this period I made myself believe that the *chlops* had been forced to kill my family; otherwise, they themselves would have been killed. Believing in the doctrine of *karma* helped me to minimize my pain and to accept my destiny – I deserved much suffering. But it did not help me to overcome anger and hurt. In fact, it eventually brought me to a place of hopelessness where I could go nowhere and I was trapped in a psychological prison of bondage. I could see nothing but darkness. How could I extricate myself from this trap?

Many years after I had lost my family, I finally convinced myself that I had overcome my past experiences. The pain that formerly affected me was now over and it no longer affected me. In fact, I was absolutely healed. I kept telling people that I was doing great. I was living in denial, but painful experiences will never subside without being faced and worked through. Denial blinded me from seeing the wounds inside my heart and prevented me from finding healing. Denial could only cause the root of unforgiveness to grow deeper into my heart and destroy my life.

For years I had been living with denial, which told me that forgiveness was hard. This denial brought nothing good into my life, only depression and bitterness. After many years of struggling to forgive, denial served as a form of covering up every emotionally painful experience that I had gone through. It helped me to survive, but it prevented me from seeing the real wounds that needed to be healed. During the first ten years after I lost my family, I did not see the connection between the past and the present. At that time, when I lived in the refugee camp in Thailand, I was absolutely lost, hopeless and depressed. When I looked at the future, I saw nothing except emotional confusion. I was not sure what I wanted in life and I had no hope of starting a new life. I consciously forced myself to believe that what had happened in the past did not affect me. When I thought about the monk who told me to bury the past so that it could not hurt me, I found this theology to be false, because I was still suffering deep pain. Darkness controlled my life and it brought only blindness to my soul.

Denial became my psychological defence mechanism. I tried to protect myself from facing what had actually happened to me, but this neither removed the pain nor taught me how to forgive. On the other hand, what could the pursuit of honour for my family give me? I could make no progress while the anger inside my heart was boiling over. During the first year after becoming a Christian, while living in Canada, I learned a passage from the Bible: 'Get rid of all bitterness, rage and anger, brawling and slander, along with every form of malice. Be kind and compassionate to one another, forgiving each other, just as in Christ God forgave you' (Ephesians 4:31–32). How could I get rid of all bitterness when I was not interested in looking at the old wounds? In fact, I did not know how to get rid of all the anger and rage in my life, because I denied its existence. However, this passage really captured my heart, even though I wasn't looking at my brokenness. I spent a lot of time reading this passage again and again.

During the many years that I was going through the spiral of anger and denial, I realized that forgiveness was a very hard truth. Indeed, because of my anger and denial, I developed a habit of being unwilling to forgive. There were five reasons why forgiveness was hard for me. First, it was hard because it was not fair that the *chlops* had killed my family; they deserved death at my hand. My mind was wrongfully programmed towards taking revenge. Nothing else had significance in my life except pursuing honour for my family by taking revenge. This was the top priority in my life, and I tried to define my own justice and my own law. If I were to let this go by forgiving the family's murderers, how could I possibly live down the shame of my failure to uphold family honour?

Secondly, forgiveness was hard because I could not just let go of the pain and the hurt in my heart and soul. It was this agony that prompted me to want to do something for my family. If I did not take vengeance, I would feel guilty about not honouring my family. The pain and hurt in my heart scolded me day after day, telling me that I was not a big man; I was a weak little man who did not have the courage to do something which would show respect for the family. This false belief kept my anger alive. How could I let go of the pain and hurt by forgiving my family's murderers?

Third, forgiveness was hard because the hurt was too great for me. I was only about thirteen years old when it had happened. I was too young to understand life. I felt as though my world had been turned upside down by the Khmer Rouge soldiers. After my family had been killed, I could never be the same again, because it had transformed my existence into darkness; I could see no future direction. Depression pursued me like a shadow and I could not get rid of it. All of life's happiness was stolen from me. My normal thinking was disrupted by restless thoughts and confused feelings. How could I forgive those people who had turned my world upside down? How could forgiveness be possible for me?

Fourth, forgiveness was hard because I was still living in bitterness. Many years after I had lost my family, I felt as though my life was still overwhelmed by the sea of bitterness which enveloped me like a flood, and there seemed no way to remove it. I became emotionally crippled and I did not know how to deal with it. I just hated the killers and cursed them that they might suffer as I had suffered. Would forgiveness help me to overcome my bitterness? How could I deal with my bitterness by forgiving them?

Finally, forgiveness was hard because no one had yet asked for forgiveness from me. I longed to hear the tormentors admit that what they had done was wrong. They must repent of the evil they had done to my family. I longed to tell them how I had felt after I had lost my family. How could I forgive when they never came to me asking for forgiveness? Could forgiveness be possible if they did not repent?

Raising these five common objections to forgiveness kept my life stationary. I hoped that now I was back in Cambodia, I could fulfil my dream of taking revenge. Yet I knew that in the pursuit of revenge I was actually digging two graves. Many good friends reminded me of that very real risk. If I wanted vengeance, I needed to be prepared to dig two graves before I went to look for the family's murderers. Even if I succeeded in killing my enemies, someone might kill me to avenge their deaths.

Therefore, I would need to dig two graves – one for me and another one for my family's killers. Vengeance would lead to an endless road of killing.

Now I can see the fruit that resulted from so much anger, bitterness, rage and hatred in my life. When this fruit took control, I was full of misery. In fact, I was burying myself deeper into a grave of bitterness and sadness. I was not aware of the powerful anger that had taken control of my life, and it began to eat me alive. Now I can hardly believe that I embraced the fruit of anger in my life for so many years. I had consciously nurtured my personal inner violence against the family's killers, but it brought me only pain and deep bitterness. It dragged my life down to the point of meaninglessness. Yet I knew I must get rid of this bitterness. I had to decide to stop the pursuit of honour for my family and to move on with a new purpose in Christ. This pursuit of honour for my family had built a wall between Christ and me. I could not get close to the Lord because the wall of my personal desire set me apart from him.

Anger helped me to live on in the hope of fulfilling my promises, but it burned me alive. It created only hatred, bitterness and disappointment, ruining my life. Nurturing anger only created relational tension with friends and others. I was afraid of communicating with people. I did not have enough confidence within myself to make friends because I just could not trust myself. Denial helped me to survive the difficult journey but its fruits were misery. It blocked me from seeing life from a Christian perspective and prevented me from seeing the glory of God through his Son's forgiveness. That forgiveness brings joy, not just for now, but eternally. I had refused to look at my wounds and seek his healing. This blocked me from accepting who I was as a person. I was hopeless and life seemed meaningless. I was diving into the grave myself and gaining nothing good in life, just moving towards emotional shutdown. I simply did not want to feel anything or to be reminded in any way of what had happened to my family.

CHAPTER FOUR

THE SHADOW OF DARKNESS

Unforgiveness brings cancer to my soul

After many years of suppression and living with anger and denial, I began to learn that I was living a life that was filled only with darkness. The root of unforgiveness was so firmly established that it was hard to remove. I was so sure that there was something wrong in my heart. I began to realize that after my family had been killed, my mind became wrongly programmed. The desire for revenge meant that I was living with an unreal dream in the hope that, one day, I would be able to fulfil my first promise. Because I wanted vengeance for my family, I unconsciously became very good at embracing my pain. I nursed it in a special place in my heart and gave it great prominence in the scheme of my life. In fact, it was my top priority.

Years of longing to take revenge created a fantasy world in my head; it was a fantasy that helped me to survive day by day. I felt I had created an image of a prison in my head, and into that prison I put the images of my family's killers. In the fifteen years since I had lost my family, every day I imagined butchering, axing, chopping and beating my family's killers in that prison. When sadness ruled in my heart, I could see myself coming into the prison to torture the killers, just to tell them that I was very angry at what they had done to my family. I just wanted to torture them so that they would suffer because of what they had done to me. I fantasized that I was an angry man who beat up these killers and made them confess to all they had done to my family, and they confessed that it was horribly wrong. Daily I visited this prison for the beating. With this daily duty of beating, torturing and chopping them up, I could control my anger. But it was not a reality; it was only my imagination and a delusion. In fact, I could not let myself out of the prison; I had locked my soul into darkness and couldn't open the prison door. I thought that I was the one in charge of this prison, but the truth was that it controlled me. I could not liberate myself from the bondage of the mental image I had created. I needed a liberator. Where could I find one?

Whenever I got upset in real life, I did not know how to deal with my feelings. Rather than deal with the real issue, I imagined that I was torturing the killers. Consequently, I had a miserable life. The *chlops* had killed my family, they had destroyed my world and made my life so painful that I hated my existence. I could not actually kill them but I could torture them in my fantasy world. Nobody ever knew that I lived with such a cruel fantasy, but it continued for years after I had lost my loved ones. The prison looked very secure; there were big iron posts keeping the images of the killers inside. They would never be given food to eat or water to drink. They deserved such cruel punishment from me and they deserved to be tortured by me every day. I realized that my cruel punishment of them was born out of hatred. This hatred created a powerful image of anger inside me, but the image took control of my life and I felt as though it burned me alive. So, although it seemed as though I had locked in the killers, in reality I was the one chained by my fantasy. I had created the delusion that kept my anger down, but it was doing me great harm.

At first I thought that I was having fun with the images of torturing, butchering, axing and chopping the family's killers, and I thought that it would satisfy my heart even though I could not actually kill them. This cruel fantasy was birthed out of my anger and hatred. I thought that doing such things in my head would make me happy and that, in a strange way, I was fulfilling my first promise. I also thought it would make me feel good to be the son that brought honour to my dead family. It would make me feel less guilty about breaking a promise I had made, but this reminded me that I had broken all three promises. I wrestled with that fact until it tormented my soul.

The awful truth was that this fantasy brought only more pain into my life, creating bitterness, hatred and anger that penetrated deeper and deeper. It helped to ease my pain for a little while, whereas it actually had a deeper long-term impact on me. Living with this cruel fantasy eventually made me miserable. The root of unforgiveness took over my life completely, and its components of hatred, anger, resentment and bitterness grew deeper into my soul until it was impossible to erase them. I had locked myself into the bondage of bitterness.

During the period of the Khmer Rouge regime, all Khmer Rouge soldiers wore black uniforms. Many years after I had lost my family, I developed an absolute hatred of black clothes. I would not wear black trousers or shirts and it bothered me when others did. When I was in my first year (1990) at Tyndale University College in Toronto, Canada, working on my bachelor's degree, I stayed in the dorm. At that time, some of the students had some black T-shirts printed with the school logo on them. They encouraged us all to wear these black T-shirts to show that we were living in the dorm. When the dorm leader gave me a black T-shirt to wear, I was angry and told him that I did not want to wear it. When he asked me why, I was silent, but a month later I asked to speak to him privately and explained to him the reason why I had not wanted to wear it. It was because of my past painful experiences with the Khmer Rouge soldiers. Black uniforms or clothes often brought back painful memories of that day when the soldiers had killed my family. After hearing my story, the dorm leader did not know what to say to me.

Many years after the loss, I learned that hatred was my natural response to the deep pain in my life, and yet it was also a deadly poison to my soul. Hatred is an unseen symptom of a deep sickness of the soul. I found it difficult to believe that hatred had so powerfully influenced my life, even though I was a Christian. Hatred robbed me of the joy I had experienced when I had first encountered the Lord, and it made me unable to see a better life ahead of me. It prevented me from making the changes that were needed if I was to regain the joy of my salvation. I could not see the future because the deadly poison in my soul blocked me from seeing the light. It made my life worse and worse and was so ugly that it was hard to admit to anyone that I hated the killers. Yet, if hatred brought nothing into my life, why did I want to embrace it? This is the most difficult question that I asked myself.

During the years of tribulation, I couldn't see a better way to live. Hatred helped me to move forward in the hope that, one day, I would be able to do something to those killers. It was a virus that infected my soul. I had once been hurt deeply, but hatred coolly ate away at my life. Eventually, it turned my existence into one great depression. This kind of depression is difficult to treat with modern medicine. I was given medication, but it did not help me at all because no doctor asked me the reason for my depression. If he had done so, I doubt if he could have helped me, as few Khmers would ever open up the wounds of their past. It is contrary to their beliefs and culture. Furthermore, the many years of unforgiveness rooted deeply within sent a signal to my heart. I eventually realized that this had become a big ball of fire consuming me alive. It was like being back in the village where we faced certain death either by starvation or torture. Again, it was not easy to die; neither was it easy to live. Many friends noticed that I was a nice fellow but that I seemed to have something hiding inside me. I was a cheerful and happy man, but my behaviour did not reflect any beauty or happiness inside my heart. I appeared to be happy, but underneath the calm exterior was the deepest pit of despair brought on by the big ball of fire that needed to be extinguished. How could I remove this stronghold that was destroying me?

I had been nurturing this burning fire inside my heart for a decade. Whenever the anger against those who had killed my family surfaced, the fire in my heart burned more severely. It affected my health and most of

Sokreaksa Himm, September 2006.

A country road approaching Siem Reap.

© Brenda Sloggett

Reaksa outside his family home at Pouk, near Siem Reap, where his sister still lives.

© Brenda Sloggett

Sokreaksa and Phaly with Philos and Sophia.

The first church built near the family home in Pouk.

The new church building at Pouk, funded by Irish supporters.

Some of the pastors leading a Bible study.
© Brenda Sloggett

The congregation after the service.

The Sunday school under the trees for shade.

Reaksa, with the man who killed his father and family:

"I gave him a Cambodian scarf as a symbol of my forgiveness, a shirt as a symbol of my love and a Bible as a symbol of my blessing…

© Brenda Sloggett

"… I also read to him from Luke 23:34: 'Jesus said, Father forgive them, for they know not what they do'."

The man who killed Reaksa's mother.

Reaksa, embracing his mother's killer, and giving him a scarf, shirt and Bible.

One year after Reaksa went to forgive his family's killers, he arranged for this school to be built. It stands as a symbol of forgiveness and hope for the future. He named it, God's Grace Primary School Kokpreach.

School dedication day, 2003. Early in 2007 it was extended by adding two further classrooms and some additional   facilities.

the time I felt sick and depressed. I could tell that something was very wrong with me, and underneath the façade I suddenly realized that I needed to forgive totally. Forgiveness is not easy, but if I allowed the big ball of fire to keep burning inside my heart, my life would not be worth living. It was hard for me to move on, but I was depressed most of the time, and this depression was the shadow of my unwillingness to forgive. When I could not forgive, I was actually burying myself into the grave of bitterness, anger and hatred. I had an image of my life being pulled apart by hatred, anger and resentment, alongside the desire to pursue my family's honour. It brought me nothing but depression.

Now I recognize that after I had lost my family I developed the characteristic symptoms of psychological distress that involved re-experiencing the traumatic events. I felt guilty about having survived while they had perished. I felt guilty about not having been able to help them. Sometimes, when I woke up in the morning, I felt sad and hopeless. Hopelessness was the greatest enemy in my life. Why had I survived? Death seemed attractive because it meant I would never feel depressed any more. Constantly, I asked myself why I wanted to live, with my world forever gone and no family left. Sadness was my daily companion and depression chased me like a shadow. There was no way out.

When I was in Toronto, Canada, I went through a period when I did not know who I was. I was profoundly lost and didn't understand myself. I was depressed, suffered headaches every day and couldn't find words to describe how I felt. Part of me was dry and empty, and every year, especially before Christmas, I felt as though I was in hell. Depression set in easily and I felt pain in my chest for at least two or three weeks in the season of hell. This was because everyone around me was talking about getting together with members of their family, and I had none. Did I know what hell was? No, but since what I had been through was what no living person should ever have to go through, I was at least entitled to label it hell. Ironically, the Cambodians called it my *karma*.

For many years I lived with nightmares and terror in my sleep. In the middle of the night, I would dream of being chased and bludgeoned by the Khmer Rouge. The images were very real to me. When I woke with a start, I couldn't fall asleep again and had to sit up for the rest of the night until morning came. My legs and hands trembled uncontrollably when I woke up. This feeling was similar to what I had experienced on the day after my family had been killed, and the terrible nightmare I had had when I was in a tree that night. An evil *chlop* was chasing me and I ran and ran to get away from him. The chase ended when I fell from the tree and woke from my nightmare. Ever since then I had had this fear, and it seemed there was no way of escape.

I had problems adjusting to everyday life and difficulties with sleeping which resulted in chronic depression. This continued for more than ten years after I had lost my family. Day after day, images from those years of torturous existence attacked my mind. I tried to control them but without success. The more I tried, the more they filled my mind. It is true that I suffered from post-traumatic stress disorder (PTSD), but I knew that the greater cause of the depression was my unwillingness to forgive my family's killers. Failure to forgive, coupled with failure to pursue justice for my family, brought depression and feelings of powerlessness. When insomnia struck me, I was very angry. After years of tribulation because of depression, I came to realize that such unwillingness to forgive also blocked me off from healing the inner hurt. I began to shut down all inner emotions.

The Bible says, 'A cheerful heart is good medicine, but a crushed spirit dries up the bones' (Proverbs 17:22). But because I was unwilling to forgive, the depression took control of my life and I had no power to control it. My life seemed dry and empty, so I learned that the road to spiritual darkness is easy, but the road to freedom in life is hard, because it involves facing inner feelings such as hurt and pain. I never wanted to look at the painful feelings. I had failed to deal with my inner feelings, so I was doomed to depression. Living such an unforgiving life for more than ten years drove me to develop distrust for others, so I forfeited the help that may have been there in the fellowship of other Christians. Unknowingly, I had chosen to be assaulted by guilt, humiliation and hopelessness, and so my capacity for intimacy with others was inhibited by intense and contradictory feelings of need and fear. The guilt I experienced was associated with my sense of shame for not being able to take revenge for my family. I was also influenced by the false Cambodian philosophy of honouring one's family by taking revenge. I felt I was a useless man.

After I had completed my bachelor's degree at Tyndale University College in 1993, I began to realize how essential forgiveness was. Although it was hard to swallow the 'garbage' that had been stuck in my throat, I had to do it, or I would always live an unhealthy life. On my own, it was very hard to forgive. How many times should I forgive? Jesus had said we should forgive 'seventy times seven', but this seemed impossible, because I was reluctant to forgive even once or twice because I had not yet cut out the root of hatred and bitterness in my heart. But my refusal to forgive meant that I never gained internal peace. The longer I remained unwilling to forgive my family's killers, the longer my spirit remained dry and my bones were burned.

I also held onto the image of the prison in my mind, venting my desire for revenge, until I realized that I could kill hundreds of *chlops*, and yet my heart would not feel satisfied. Perhaps I could bomb a whole village and kill all the people, yet still it would not be enough. In failing to forgive, I lost my peace of mind, and my resentment grew into a ball of fire that settled in my heart and continually burned me. The fire was so big that it was beyond my emotional ability to extinguish it.

Thus, not only had I failed to forgive my family's murderers, but I had also failed to take care of my own life and health. I was blind to the fact that unforgiveness was the cancer of my soul which brought only a process of slow death. I had failed to see my life being strangled by a giant rope of hatred, anger, bitterness and disappointment. It was impossible to move on in my own strength. This rope had destroyed my life and health. I would never find peace and restoration until this rope of negative emotions was cut off. Things started to change only when I took a hard look at what I had long ignored – my lack of forgiveness. It had damaged my life enough. I needed to let it go and start living again.

Hebrew 12:15 warns, 'See to it that no one misses the grace of God and that no bitter root grows up to cause trouble and defile many.' The failure to forgive had blinded me from seeing the grace of God in my life. In fact, I resisted the healing grace of God by living my life in the bondage of toxic emotions: hatred, anger, bitterness and resentment. Nothing could remove such emotions from my life – except forgiveness. I now know the consequences of allowing a root of unforgiveness to grow in one's heart. Its effect is deadly. It took me many years to realize how the bitterness, sadness and anger had taken control of my life. I had to make a deliberate act of the will to remove it; otherwise it would have permanently damaged my emotional, spiritual, physical and psychological being. Eventually, it would destroy my whole life's happiness. Life would never bring me joy, only darkness. From this moment on, I must rely on the healing power of the Holy Spirit and his help to extinguish that big ball of fire in my heart.

Unforgiveness brings the deepest darkness into one's life, and although I had been a Christian for more than five years, my life had not been transformed from darkness to light because I could not forgive. This darkness not only hurt me but also blinded me from seeing the gift of God. God first forgave me, and he asks me to forgive others who sin against me:

> Anyone who claims to be in the light but hates his brother is still in the darkness. Whoever loves his brother lives in the light, and there is nothing in him to make him stumble. But whoever hates his brother is in the darkness and walks around in the darkness; he does not know where he is going, because the darkness has blinded him. (1 John 2:9–11)

This passage challenged my unforgiving character. I had nowhere to go, except darkness. Hatred, anger, bitterness and depression are signs of spiritual darkness, and holding on to these had blinded me from seeing the grace of God in my life. They had blinded me from seeing my own bondage to darkness.

Looking back at the years of darkness, I could see many reasons why I had been unable to forgive. First, I had not been able to forgive because it was not fair to my family. How could I forgive such evil people? Now I realized that I was failing to let God be the judge. I just wanted to be my own judge. I wanted justice to be done in my way. Paul instructs us:

> Do not repay anyone evil for evil. Be careful to do what is right in the eyes of everybody. If it is possible, as far as it depends on you, live at peace with everyone. Do not take revenge, my friends, but leave room for God's wrath, for it is written: 'It is mine to avenge; I will repay,' says the Lord. (Romans 12:17–19)

I had failed to allow God to be the righteous judge. Vengeance is the Lord's, not mine. He will do it in his own way and in his own time. I should not be involved in his business, because he is the righteous judge and no evil escapes his all-seeing eyes.

'It is a dreadful thing to fall into the hands of the living God' (Hebrews 10:31). I had escaped the judgment to come by receiving Christ as my Saviour, but if the killers did not repent, they would face the coming judgment, which is a terrible future.

Secondly, I had not been able to forgive because I had refused to let go of the hurt. How could I let go of the hurt when I could not forgive? This question helped me to see my inner struggle and helped me to understand that I was failing to see the richest grace in my life. '"Their sins and lawless acts I will remember no more."

And where these have been forgiven, there is no longer any sacrifice for sin' (Hebrews 10:17–18). God does not remember my sins any more. God had forgiven me and had cancelled all my sins, but I had failed to let go of the sins of my family's killers!

Thirdly, I had not been able to forgive because I had lost so much of my life. But, actually, wasn't I failing to see how big my sin was when God forgave me? I could see only the sins of others. God had forgiven my giant sin, but I had failed to forgive others. Jesus once told this story about an unforgiving servant:

> Therefore, the kingdom of heaven is like a king who wanted to settle accounts with his servants. As he began the settlement, a man who owed him ten thousand talents was brought to him. Since he was not able to pay, the master ordered that he and his wife and his children and all that he had be sold to repay the debt.
>
> The servant fell on his knees before him. 'Be patient with me,' he begged, 'and I will pay back everything.' The servant's master took pity on him, cancelled the debt and let him go.
>
> But when that servant went out, he found one of his fellow servants who owed him a hundred denarii. He grabbed him and began to choke him. 'Pay back what you owe me!' he demanded.
>
> His fellow servant fell to his knees and begged him, 'Be patient with me, and I will pay you back.'
>
> But he refused. Instead, he went off and had the man thrown into prison until he could pay the debt. (Matthew 18:23–30)

Thoroughly examining this passage, I could see that I was like this poor fellow who could not forgive his friend just a small debt. At the end, he was locked in prison. God never locked me in prison, but I consciously locked myself in the prison of unforgiveness. My self-pity insisted on demanding retribution when I thought about all I had lost. This thinking did not allow me to go anywhere. I embraced my loss, and it locked my life into the scenario of unforgiveness. Not only did I fail to let Jesus Christ transform my life, but I also failed to see that God first forgave my giant sins, and he says I must forgive those who sin against me.

Fourthly, I had not been able to forgive because I was embracing my bitterness. I had failed to open my wounds for healing. Embracing bitterness, I chained myself to the dark side of life. 'For I see that you are full of bitterness and captive to sin' (Acts 8:23). I had failed to get rid of it and start my life again. I had allowed my bitterness to take deep root in my soul, and it had ruined my personal relationship with the Lord. It had prevented me from seeing his beauty and grace. It had created a cancer in my soul. I had waited far too long before realizing that my bitterness was eating my life away. I had allowed bitterness to spring up in my life. 'See to it that no one misses the grace of God and that no bitter root grows up to cause trouble and defile many' (Hebrews 12:15). Bitterness had blocked my vision of the beauty of healing from the Lord. The spirit of unforgiveness had locked me into bitterness and darkness.

Fifthly, I had not been able to forgive because I had been expecting the family's killers to come and ask me for forgiveness. 'Father, forgive them, for they do not know what they are doing' (Luke 23:34). Jesus did not expect those who crucified him to approach him to ask for forgiveness, yet he asked his heavenly Father to forgive them.

My expectation had led me to live my life in hostility to others and I had failed to live at peace. Paul wrote: 'If it is possible, as far as it depends on you, live at peace with everyone' (Romans 12:18). What would life bring me if I kept holding onto my own expectations? Nothing but darkness. Paul also said:

> Live in peace with each other. And we urge you, brothers, warn those who are idle, encourage the timid, help the weak, be patient with everyone. Make sure that nobody pays back wrong for wrong, but always try to be kind to each other and to everyone else. (1 Thessalonians 5:14-15)

Forgiveness does not liberate other people from me but, rather, I am choosing to liberate myself from the bondage of bitterness. I had to summon all my emotional energy to examine the hurt in my past and move on with a new purpose in life. This was a road of personal transformation from darkness into light. I had to allow myself to be transformed by the Holy Spirit, for my stubborn heart had created only darkness in my soul. It brought spiritual damage to my life and kept me from worshipping God joyfully.

I began to realize that nothing in life is beyond forgiveness, as long as I am willing to rely on the grace of God to overcome my own darkness. I realized that I needed to make time and be willing to accept God's grace in travelling this road. It is contrary to human nature, but it will lead me to see the beauty of life beyond forgiveness. I realized I had to make a decision to be liberated from the bondage of hurt, anger, bitterness and hatred that had crippled my life. I had seen the cancer in my soul and needed to remove it so that it could not spread deeper into my life. I had seen the darkness that resulted from my emotional blindness. My conviction of forgiveness was birthed out of my self-awareness – it required a degree of self-love and self-care. I needed to look seriously at my emotional, physical and spiritual self.

But had I forgotten the cross of Christ? My mind had to refocus on the pivotal teaching of the Christian faith – that of free forgiveness, because Jesus gave up his sinless life to redeem me and bring me into the family of God. Belonging to this family was the greatest gift he had given me, but my enjoyment of this great privilege was destroyed when I harboured an unforgiving spirit. If he says we must forgive, how can we refuse such a wonderful Saviour this small request? His sufferings were beyond any human comprehension, but I knew my life belonged to him and I must obey his commands if I was to grow in my Christian faith. I began to focus on the cross and all it had meant to my Lord, and this helped me to put my pain into perspective.

I had spent a lot of time trying to discover how to live my life while pursuing my first promise to avenge my family. Unconsciously, I had invested time and energy focusing on what I should do to achieve this. As I struggled, I made myself even more angry, resentful and bitter. These destructive emotions slipped into my life and made me very negative. Looking to my past led me nowhere; my future was filled with darkness, hopelessness and bitterness. Now, I needed to look forward to a new life in Christ; God had given me a second chance to live. Forgiveness could liberate me from these destructive emotions.

Only this message can save the hurting people of Cambodia.

CHAPTER FIVE

FORGIVENESS

The art of overcoming the shadow of darkness

If I were rich, it would have been easier for me to donate a million dollars to an orphanage than to say 'I forgive you' to those who had killed my family. The long-drawn-out pursuit of my family's honour had sapped my emotional energy. Then an old friend's experience helped me to see what I needed to do. A few years ago, I had helped him cut down a mango tree near his house. Years before, he had eaten mangoes and thrown the seeds everywhere around his house. One seed happened to sprout near the house. At first, he had thought that the young plant would not cause any problems. He was not interested in cutting down the young tree, because he looked forward to the time when he would enjoy eating its fruit every year. It did not occur to him that he would have trouble later. Many years passed by, and the tree's roots began to damage the concrete of the house. He still thought that he would not need to cut down the tree for a long time. Years later, when the house was about to collapse he started worrying about it. By then, it was too late for him to deal with the problem by himself. The tree was too big for him to cut down alone, and he was too weak to handle it even if he had been able to cut it down. Actually, my friend's story reflected my problem many years ago when I could not forgive. I could see that the root of unforgiveness was so big and firm in my life that I would never be able to cut it down in my own strength. I needed God's help to pull out the root. I wished I could have been given some kind of electric shock therapy to remove that root of unforgiveness so that I would not need to face the pain of learning to forgive, but no such thing exists in this world. Forgiveness does not work in such a way.

I could not straddle two boats; if I tried to do so, I would fall into the water. I had to decide which route to choose in order to keep moving forward: the old life, that of unforgiveness and the pursuit of my family's honour; or my new life of faith and hope in Jesus Christ. Freedom was granted to me to choose, but I had to decide which route I would take. Far from being an easy decision for me to make, this was a painful choice. Few people want to face facts like this. It seemed easier to live with the root of unforgiveness than to swallow a garbage bag that I had never deserved.

Having been a Christian for five years, I had learned a lot about forgiveness, but my heart had not absorbed its significance. I had learned from people and books, but it was hard to put this teaching into practice. I had the freedom to choose to forgive, but I then needed to ask a lot of questions. How could I forgive those who killed my family? What does forgiveness mean to me? Will forgiving lead me to forget? Is it possible to forget, and if so, how? As I struggled with these questions, my understanding of forgiveness grew, and I saw that forgiveness could become an internal psychological revolution against life's injustices. I realized that forgiveness is not an easy work to carry out, but I could not live my life with the root of unforgiveness. I had to let it go.

When I became a Christian in 1990, thirteen years had elapsed since my family's deaths in Cambodia. During those years I had lived with anger, resentment and bitter hatred. My life was characterized by the emotions directly associated with the cruelty and injustice of their deaths. The events that took place in the forest in 1977 were still as fresh in my mind as they had been on that day; it was the pivotal point of my life. But now I had experienced another pivotal event in my life: I had come to know Jesus as my Saviour and Lord. Through the redeeming blood of Jesus, my sins were forgiven and I had eternal life. When I committed my life to Christ, I knew that he alone could fully understand my pain, because he had suffered for me on a cruel cross. He knew my path. Knowing Jesus gave me peace in my heart, and my life began to take on a new direction.

I knew that the deadly pursuit of my family's honour had brought me no satisfaction; it had destroyed my health, my peace of mind and my spiritual relationship with the Lord. During the first few years of my Christian life, pain, bitterness and depression ruled me and I knew little about Christian joy. I knew that I had to do things that were impossible in my own meagre strength, but by relying on God's grace I could learn to forgive and live in newness of life with Christ.

While learning to forgive, I became aware that this meant dealing with the stages of rage, anger, bitterness, hurt and depression. No step could be omitted, and the question of whether forgiving meant also forgetting was a major problem for me. I had grown up in a culture that taught me suppression. It taught me to bury the past and forget it. However, that did not allow me to move on in my Christian life. I found it impossible to forget, but forgiveness is not forgetting. By forgiving those who killed my family I have not erased the painful experiences from my heart and memory. They will always be part of me, as no one forgets someone whom they have loved and lost. The images of them being clubbed to death remain. Real forgiveness takes place when I am willing to accept the secondary pain. These are the painful memories that I can only submit to the cross of Christ. His love and compassion have taken my life out of darkness. Few humans can understand my feelings and the unspeakable horrors I have seen that still haunt me in nightmares, but I am responsible for choosing my own freedom that will heal my wounds. I am responsible for taking the broken pieces of the puzzle that makes my life and putting them back together.

On one occasion I shared my pain with friends and asked them, 'What does forgiveness mean?' They had no answer but suggested that I get in touch with my bitterness, and then they walked away. I was searching for the significance of forgiveness, but perhaps they had never had experiences in life that hurt them deeply. They had never been in my shoes, so how could they understand bitterness? They meant well, but they had only head knowledge and no real experience in their hearts. There I was, crying out to understand the full meaning of forgiveness, and they had no idea of the pain and hurt that was within me. This reminded me of Job and the bitterness of soul he experienced when his friends could not understand his pain.

When you have been deeply hurt, the journey through such pain takes time. Fifteen years passed before I learned to forgive. When I was young, my father used to tell me, 'Don't take advantage of people by telling them to do something that you have never been through. You have no idea how difficult it is. Don't tell others to do something that you do not intend to learn.' His words reinforced what I had learned through my friends. The school of preaching is easier than the school of practice. It is easy to teach people, but we must first put our theories into practice. I have sought to apply my father's advice to the need of forgiveness. We know the teachings of Jesus to forgive those who have sinned against us, but few have had to deal with the terrible tragedy that was mine.

One of the problems of counselling is that those who seek to counsel sometimes do not seek to know all the details of the pain in the one they are helping. If they did, such counsellors might themselves realize how difficult it is to forgive. It takes time to go through emotional rebuilding, and they must be willing to go through the traumatic events in the life of the damaged person. I had tried for years to forget the events, without success. Forgiveness does not work that way. When I tried to suppress all the traumas, it built up tension within and the bitterness, hatred and anger resurfaced. Forgiveness necessitated walking through the past traumas and then making a decision to paint a new future with Christ. I had been a Christian for almost five years before I could see the road towards forgiveness. It is a long journey of healing emotional pain, and only I could take this road.

I made a decision to take this journey so that it would enhance my relationship with the Lord Jesus Christ and lead me to overcome the bitterness with his power and strength. This gave me a new purpose in life.

I still had to learn to overcome the terrible memories of the way my family had been butchered, but by relying on the power of the Holy Spirit, I could know complete healing. The grace of God helped me to remove the root of unforgiveness that had been in my heart for such a long period of time. I listed every aspect of the past experiences that had wounded me so deeply, and I could see that these legacies were crippling my relationships with the Lord and with other people around me. Paul says:

> Do not repay anyone evil for evil. Be careful to do what is right in the eyes of everybody. If it is possible, as far as it depends on you, live at peace with everyone. Do not take revenge, my friends, but leave room for God's wrath, for it is written: 'It is mine to avenge; I will repay,' says the Lord. (Romans 12:17–19)

The apostle is right, and I will not repay evil for evil. It is not my business, neither am I qualified to do this. If I were allowed to take revenge, it would not satisfy me, neither could forgiveness be shown in this way. I asked myself whether killing the murderers to satisfy my desire for revenge would be the electric-shock treatment I longed for, which would erase the memories of pain. But I knew nothing would erase the memories. As I sought to apply this passage to my life, I realized that I had to accept that I would not repay evil for evil. This was the essential point of my understanding of forgiveness. I had to force myself to accept my pain until it became my own personal psychological revolution against life's injustices. It wasn't fair that I had endured so much, neither was it fair that my family had been killed. But demanding my justice would never bring back what I had lost. Using my natural anger to deal with the evil things that had been done to my family would never eliminate hatred from my heart, but instead it would increase the fire of anger and it would also lead me into a life of self-destructive behaviour.

Forgiveness had to come from my own moral conscience and I needed liberty to release myself from the bondage of bitterness. I had to keep my life moving on with Christ and his all-sufficient grace. This was journeying towards healing and wiping away the tears of my soul. This decision to forgive was difficult, but it enabled me to remove the roots of bitterness, anger and hatred, and so to move forward to a better life. God was waiting to show me that, through forgiveness, I would be healed. I was so tired of carrying my pain, and these emotions robbed me of freedom. I had become a slave to that root of unforgiveness and I had no peace. Hurt and pain demanded that I settle the score for my family; they hooked me on the pursuit of honour, and hatred blocked me from loving other people. Anger and resentment had tormented me into creating the fantasy in my head in which I was to be a kind of 'Terminator'. Bitterness had robbed me of the joy of life and had trapped me in the darkness. My unforgiving spirit had stolen my freedom.

I had gained nothing from these negative emotions and now I needed to open my wounds to the healing power of the Holy Spirit. I realized that God had first forgiven me without my plea for forgiveness, so I must forgive them even though they did not seek forgiveness from me. When forgiveness came from my own free will, it freed the killers from the place they occupied in my mind. I used to believe that forgiveness set my family's killers free from their obligation to me. That was untrue. Now I realized that forgiveness was, rather, the willingness to set myself free from the bondage of bitterness. I had to break the bondage of all that had imprisoned me in the Killing Fields experience, and then be the kind of person that God wanted me to be. Nothing is impossible with God, so by his grace I humbled myself and asked for his help to extinguish the fire of hatred and anger inside my heart.

One night in early 1994, I knelt down and prayed: 'Lord God, I have tasted enough bitterness in my life. I know that the root of unforgiveness is very deep in my heart and soul. Because I avoided pulling it out earlier, it has now taken a deep root. The big ball of fire has burned me day after day, and the pictures of the killers are in my mind all the time. I have no peace, only hatred, anger and bitterness, and these are bearing rotten fruit. My life is unhealthy. It is enough for me to make this final decision to forgive. Father God, I ask you to grant me power to root out the unforgiveness that has grown in my heart and soul for years. Grant me peace and clean my heart as I forgive those who killed my family. From now on, Father God, I set them free from my heart, and I ask you, God, to heal my wounds, forgive me and give me a new heart.'

After I had said this prayer, tears flowed down my face. I could not hold on to my emotions any more, and didn't want to, for I was crying tears of relief. The impossible mission had been fulfilled. I had made a decision to cancel the pursuit of the killers, and I no longer wanted them to suffer as I had done, neither had I any desire to make them pay the price they deserved. This prayer had changed my life in a very positive way. It helped me to open my wounds for healing. It healed the cancer of my soul. It brought hope to my life. It helped me to see my bright future.

At long last I had forgiven my family's killers and set them free from my mental imagery. I had chosen to remove the roots of bitterness, hatred, anger and resentment from my heart and to live my life with a new purpose in Christ. I chose to build up my relationship with God and to prepare myself to accept the grace of healing from the Lord. Finally I made a deliberate choice to obey my Lord's teaching.

After I had said this prayer, my life was not transformed overnight. I had taken the first step on that long road of forgiveness, and I was journeying towards healing. I trusted God to give me the strength to persevere. I knew in my heart that he could accomplish this work in me. In the process of learning to forgive, I spent a lot of time reading the following passage. I probably read this scripture more than a hundred times as I dug out the reasons to forgive:

> Get rid of all bitterness, rage and anger, brawling and slander, along with every form of malice. Be kind and compassionate to one another, forgiving each other, just as in Christ God forgave you. Be imitators of God, therefore, as dearly loved children and live a life of love, just as Christ loved us and gave himself up for us as a fragrant offering and sacrifice to God. (Ephesians 4:31 – 5:2)

After meditating on this passage for several days, I identified five reasons why I had forgiven my family's murderers. First, I had to forgive because I needed to start life again. I had had enough bitterness in my life and needed to move on, because Christ had given me a new purpose. I could no longer allow myself to be infected by the cancer of my soul, or it would destroy me. Life should be a joyful journey in Christ, so I had to remove all the negative emotions that had made me so miserable. The road to emotional healing was not always easy. It demanded my emotional energy to rely on the grace of God to cut down all negative feelings. I needed to see my bright future through the grace of God. I could never start again if I were not determined to cut down all the negative emotions that had ruled my life.

Secondly, I had to forgive because I needed to live my life to glorify God. How could I bring glory to God when I was hiding such bitterness inside my heart? How could I have a good relationship with the Lord when I lived my life in the sea of bitterness? Jesus said, 'Love the Lord your God with all your heart and with all your soul and with all your mind. This is the first and greatest commandment' (Matthew 22:37–38). It was hard to love the Lord when bitterness ruled my life. I remembered how I had gone to church for the first four years of my Christian life with bitterness in my heart. I had no joy in worshipping the Lord. One good friend who knew me well and had spent a lot of time learning about me, took the risk one day of challenging me. 'Reaksa, I do not think you are happy,' he said. 'I have observed your behaviour and I can tell that there is some bitterness in your life.' He had hit the nail on the head. I could hardly accept what my friend had said to me, because his words had caused deep pain. Truth hurts, but failing to face it hurts more. I had to learn to accept it.

Now I was determined to remove the root of bitterness so that I could freely glorify God in my life. I believe God smiles at me when I glorify him cheerfully and whole heartedly. Forgiveness is not an option for me, but a free choice to glorify God by living a healthy lifestyle. Paul exhorted Christians to get rid of bitterness, anger and rage because these negative emotions bring nothing good in life. They destroyed my relationship with the Lord and prevented me from communing with him. How could I have joy when I was full of bitterness? How could I love the Lord with all my heart, soul and strength when I nurtured hatred? In this state I could not worship God. True worship must be genuine and heartfelt, not just pretence and fake. God is not pleased with my praising lips when my heart is not right with him. Therefore, forgiving my family's murderers was the only way I could make room for God's love to purify my heart, and the one route to praise and glorify him with joy.

I was tired of living my old life, paralysed by the cancer of my soul. Now I wanted to begin afresh. Life is fragile and short: one day I will die. I wanted to live the remaining chapters of my life freely in Christ. David once prayed, 'Show me, O Lord, my life's end and the number of my days; let me know how fleeting is my life' (Psalm 39:4). Knowing that my stay on earth was temporary made me realize how much I wanted to live my life for Christ. I knew that the issue of forgiveness was the barrier for me, and I wanted to overcome it. I wanted to write in my heart a sentence about the last chapter of my life: 'I have forgiven my family's murderers. I can do so by the grace of God.'

Before I was able to forgive, I had had no joy in worshipping God and had been robbed of the joy of life;

bitterness had seeped into my bones. How could I worship the Lord my God with joy when my life was crippled by bitterness? The first and greatest commandment that Jesus gave is 'Love the Lord your God with all your heart and with all your soul and with all your mind and with all your strength' (Mark 12:30). I cannot love the Lord my God when my heart is poisoned by bitterness. God is not pleased with me if I cannot forgive. I must forgive so that I can worship him with joy in life.

Thirdly, I had to forgive to pass on what I had freely received. God has forgiven my countless sins, so I must possess the spirit of forgiveness that he gives me. Therefore, I need to forgive sincerely, even as God forgives my countless sins. At church, how could I pray, 'Forgive us our sins, as we forgive those who sin against us'? Sometimes, I felt as though I was insane to say such a wonderful prayer. On some occasions, because I could not say it sincerely from my heart, I just pretended to say this prayer. It was not sincere. Forgiveness demands an act of obedience to the Lord. It is his command, and this is not optional, nor must I take his command lightly; I must live in obedience to him. As I thought deeply about this, I thoroughly examined the Bible, and couldn't find a single account of where men first approached God for forgiveness. Rather, God first forgave men without any initiative from them. God's character is full of love and compassion. He sent his Son to die for our sins, which was something we could never deserve. Most of us fail to remember that we were forgiven first, so if we fail to transfer this gift of grace to others, it adds to the many simple mistakes that Christians have made throughout history.

We are reminded of the unforgiving servant whom

Jesus talked about in Matthew 18:24-35. According to this passage, the main theme is the cancelling of the debt or the loan that the servant owed to his master. The pitfall in our generation is that we too have failed to forgive others, just as the unforgiving servant failed to forgive his fellow man. For example, in Western society, when things go wrong – for example, when a marriage crisis arises – people often deal with it by hiring a lawyer to settle the problem with their spouse. Forgiveness brings beauty to life, but failing to forgive brings only darkness. This story of the unforgiving servant reminds me of how, for years, I had wanted to butcher my family's murderers. I was just like that unforgiving servant! Forgiveness is a gift from God, but this gift can only be seen through human demonstration. Such demonstration reflects the character of our Lord Jesus Christ – he is the forgiving God. My ability to forgive is birthed out of my awareness of the grace of God in my life.

Fourthly, I had to forgive because I must imitate my Lord's example. I call Jesus my Lord and Master, so I must obey him. His forgiveness demands an act of obedience. God forgave me, so I have to be willing to forgive others. 'Forgive us our debts, as we also have forgiven our debtors' (Matthew 6:12). We must not take this command lightly. As I reflect on this truth, one picture becomes so vivid in my mind. When Jesus hung on that cruel cross, he did not wait for those who had nailed his hands and feet to ask for forgiveness. His pain must have been immense, but he said, 'Father, forgive them, for they do not know what they are doing' (Luke 23:34). I think that this is the most powerful and essential message of forgiveness. I do not need to endure the physical pain that he endured, but what I can do is imitate his example of forgiveness, because he is my Saviour, my Master, my Lord and my God. My act of obedience has to reflect the character of the Lord.

The debt I owe to God – my Creator and Saviour – is so great that I could never pay it back even if I lived a hundred lifetimes. The debt that the killers owed me – just another human – could never be as great as my debt to God, no matter what they did. For a long time, even though I had become a Christian, I failed to see how God had forgiven me so freely, or what the consequence was: that I had a responsibility to forgive those who had injured me. I had failed to offer this gift of grace to others. Instead, I had thrown my tormentors into the prison of my mind, where I kept them until I could find a way of getting my revenge. I wanted to force them to atone for what they had done, if necessary by paying with their lives.

Finally, I had to forgive in order to demonstrate God's love to my enemies. The message of loving our enemies is the most fundamental teaching of Jesus Christ. He said, 'Love your enemies, do good to those who hate you, bless those who curse you, pray for those who ill-treat you' (Luke 6:27–28). I came to realize that, to love my family's killers, I had to forgive them. This is a difficult and painful love. Not only had my enemies hated me, cursed me and treated me cruelly; they tried to kill me, and they succeeded in killing my family. They turned my world upside down, and tore away everything I had ever known and loved. I was thirteen years old. Now I am a man, but I still carry the memory and pain of what they did to me. Would it ever be possible to love them?

I chose to forgive my family's killers, because I realized that I could not live with the root of unforgiveness in my life that prevented me from freely living with others. If I consciously choose to live my life with an unsettled account, I choose to be a loser. Cambodians are fond of saying, 'The winner will go to evil's side, but the loser will go to God's side.' This saying signifies that the loser will choose to sleep in peace, because he accepts his loss, but the winner will create more internal fear. He will be restless. Forgiveness is not to gain back what was initially lost, but to live with the loss by relying on the grace of God to overcome the hurt and pain in life.

I chose to start over again and I chose to cancel what I actually wanted to do to them many years ago. I chose to stop pursuing honour for my family. I chose to replace hate with love. I chose to learn to love my family's killers. I chose healing for the wounds I had endured for many years. This is a hard road to travel and not many people are willing to travel it. We are all responsible for the choices we make. If we choose to disobey God, we will reap the consequences of doing that, but if we choose to obey, we will have a harvest of peace and joy. I must continually rely on the grace of God so that I can travel this road with peace and serenity. I must forgive because I do not want the smouldering fire of my soul to consume my life and eventually destroy it. I do not want to wait until it is too late to forgive.

The good news is that by the grace of God, everything is possible. Indeed, by loving my tormentors I can be liberated from the pain of my past; forgiveness gives me the freedom to move on. The message of love for my enemies transforms my life – from being paralysed by the power of hatred, I am now free in Christ. I am a new person, a dearly loved child of God. Since Christ loves me, I can pass on that love to my enemies.

Does forgiving mean forgetting? How can I ever forget my family? Does forgiving depend on how I feel? How can I summon the emotional energy to face the task of forgiving? Is forgiveness as easy as some people make it sound? In forgiving, I chose to start my life again. The grace of God helped me to let go of the pursuit of my family's honour, and in this way it was the spiritual power that eventually broke the tie that bound the killers to my soul. I cannot forget my family, nor am I expected to. I grew up in a Buddhist culture that encourages people to suppress their emotions, but the road that God has led me into has at last brought me peace, contentment and joy.

Choosing to face the hurts was part of an internal process of healing, and putting forgiveness into practice was part of this process. I am reminded of the time when Peter came to Jesus and asked, 'Lord, how many times shall I forgive my brother when he sins against me? Up to seven times?' Jesus replied, 'I tell you, not seven times, but seventy times seven' (Matthew 18:21–22). I believe that Peter was stunned by Jesus' command to forgive so many times. Forgiveness is not a quantitative thing. It is qualitative. The heart must be willing to let the injustice go. If we say we forgive a million times but our heart still embraces the hurt, this means we do not really forgive. Jesus knew that forgiveness would not be easy for us. It takes time and emotional energy to work through past hurts. The ultimate demand of forgiveness is to ask the muscles of the soul to work through every bitter emotion. There is nothing pleasant about this, but it is like a painkiller that eventually removes the pain. In my case, I had to make that choice of swallowing that unwanted legacy and understanding that God forgives mistakes. A forgiving attitude is essential for well-being, and after putting all these things into practice, I experienced healing of the soul. Forgiveness is holy medicine from God, and I needed it badly. It is as refreshing as a heavy rain.

Twelve years after forgiving my family's killers (in 1994), I observe that my life has changed dramatically. I am healthier than I was and the depression has left me. I no longer need tranquillizers because the Prince of Peace rules my life. My mind is at peace and the joy of life has been restored. The prison door of my heart has been broken open, hatred has been uprooted and bitterness has been washed away by the water of life from the Holy Spirit. 'For I will forgive their wickedness and will remember their sins no more' (Hebrews 8:12). The fire of anger has subsided and I am at peace. I have found that it is impossible to remove the anger at what the killers did, but I have learned to overcome its power. It no longer affects my life, nor can it make me miserable. The grace of God has enabled me to live in joy and peace once more. I tell people that even after forgiving my family's killers, I still get angry. Anger is the executive power of human emotion, and if I had no anger at the injustices and evils in our world, there would be something wrong with me. So I can still get angry, but I no longer hate the killers and I have received healing of the wounds of my past.

A little while ago, I was invited to speak at a Christian health conference run by World Vision in Cambodia. I was asked to speak from a Cambodian mental-health perspective, and afterwards, many people asked questions about anger and forgiveness. One person asked, 'Can someone who has forgiven an offender cease to feel angry?'

A medical doctor on the panel answered, 'If you truly forgive an offender, you will no longer feel angry. Take Reaksa, for example. He took many years to forgive his family's killers, but now he does not get angry any more. If you gave him a punch, he would not get angry with you.'

I was shocked. When I stood up to reply, I told the audience that while I respected this doctor's views, I had to disagree with him. It is true that I have forgiven the Khmer Rouge killers, but I am still angry about the evil that was done in those days. If I were not to feel anger any more, I would have lost part of my humanity. If you punched me, of course I would feel angry with you – but my anger is manageable and I can live with it. It does not lead me to hate or to do evil things, or even to punch you in return. Paul said, 'In your anger do not sin. Do not let the sun go down while you are still angry' (Ephesians 4:26). What I have learned from this verse is that getting angry is not bad in itself – it is a normal human emotion. It is only failing to manage your anger that is bad; it can damage your life and ruin your relationship with God. After I had delivered this message, the audience was silent. I assume they had been thinking that after forgiveness, no one should feel angry any more, because expressing anger is not acceptable in Cambodian society.

I see the grace of God in my life. I know that forgiveness is the spiritual power that breaks the chains that bind me. It quenches the fire of bitterness and digs out the roots of anger. I have been released from the emotional bondage that hampered me for years. Not only have I forgiven the killers, I have also forgiven myself for holding onto those negative emotions for so long. In many ways, I was torturing myself by insisting on living in that dark place of anger and bitterness. By forgiving myself, I have been liberated from the power of psychological guilt. It took courage to look at my brokenness and say, 'I am sorry for hurting myself for so long. I regret how I have damaged myself.' That is my personal liberation. And all this I owe to the work of God's grace in my heart.

Years ago when I was in Canada, after I had addressed the audience on forgiveness, a young girl asked, 'Reaksa, what would you do if you were to meet your family's killers?' It was one of the most important questions I have ever faced in my life. I would never have expected a child to ask me such a question. It was not easy for me to answer. However, I took courage and replied, 'I would forgive them.' It was the first time I had said this in public. After this, whenever I spoke in public, I gave the same message, and this brought about a longing within my soul to meet the killers and be finally reconciled. Forgiveness takes one person to do the job, but reconciliation takes both sides. Thus far, I had only done my side of the business.

CHAPTER SIX

RECONCILIATION

After the heavy rain,
the sky becomes clear again

Reconciliation can never take place if forgiveness is not granted first. No one could wake up one morning and decide to search for their family's killers and then begin to build a relationship with them. I think it would be relatively easy for one of us to deliver a message of forgiveness to a far-distant offender, but coming face to face with them would be an entirely different scenario, especially when the offence was so grave. It took me years to consider reconciliation, and I always doubted whether it would ever be achieved. There were so many thoughts and stress-provoking issues filling my head. I was not sure what I would do and what I would say if I met them and tried to be reconciled. They were murderers, and they murdered my closest family members. But now I was beginning this journey towards reconciliation, and it was a scary prospect. I had no idea what to expect.

Making the decision to meet with them created tremendous uncertainty in my life, because I did not know what the outcome would be. I wondered if they might kill me, because they thought I had come to take revenge. However, I was strongly determined to fulfil my mission of forgiveness, so I set up three specific goals to prepare myself: (1) Build up good prayer support, clearly setting out my expectations for the trip. (2) Take the necessary courage and face them. (3) Tell them I had forgiven them.

A few months before I made the trip, I wrote a number of emails to friends, asking them to pray about it. Many friends wrote to me and encouraged me to stand firm with the Lord. In addition to the prayer support, I received much moral and emotional support. The trip's outcome would be unpredictable, but I was determined to meet the killers. How I would react to them when I actually faced them, I didn't know. Just thinking about it gave me shivers in my stomach. These were my family's killers and the prospect of meeting them was daunting. Only through prayer, moral and emotional support would this become a reality.

My primary expectation from the trip was simply to meet them, and I knew it would be foolish to expect anything from them, but I could only make my mission of forgiveness complete if we met. It is very unusual for Cambodian people to say, 'I'm sorry', so I didn't expect an apology. I wanted to tell them that I had come to cancel my revenge and set them free from me. They would not need to fear me in the future because I no longer wished they were dead, but rather, I wanted them to be blessed. I had come to make peace and build a relationship with them, not to make war. This may sound simple and easy, but in fact this goal was difficult for me. I knew I had to rely on the strength of the Lord, but I wondered how I would be able to articulate the words of forgiveness. I knew it was a difficult road, but I intended to accomplish my mission.

The night before the arranged meeting, I was unable to sleep. I tossed and turned, and my stomach was sickened by the prospect before me. My deepest emotions were stirred and in turmoil. So I rose at 3:30 a.m., opened my Bible and flipped from one page to another to find a good passage to read in preparation for the trip. I stopped at 2 Corinthians 5:18–21:

> All this is from God, who reconciled us to himself through Christ and gave us the ministry of reconciliation: that God was reconciling the world to himself in Christ, not counting men's sins against them. And he has committed to us the message of reconciliation. We are therefore Christ's ambassadors, as though God were making his appeal through us. We implore you on Christ's behalf: Be reconciled to God. God made him who had no sin to be sin for us, so that in him we might become the righteousness of God.

This passage seemed like God speaking to me, reminding me that I was an ambassador for Christ. I knelt down and prayed for the courage to go to meet the killers and for protection from my Lord. My prayer was very simple. I just prayed exactly how I felt and told God of my frustration, anger, hurt, insecurity and resentment. After two hours of praying like this, I felt peace about my trip and was ready to travel the long journey, to meet them, forgive them and to be reconciled. If I could not become reconciled with them, I felt as though my forgiveness would not be complete. If I had been asked to do this twenty years ago, I would have refused; now I knew I had to take this journey. I was doing it for my own sake and in obedience to my Lord's commands. Nobody else would do it for me. I also felt that God was taking me a step further in my faith and that he wanted me to seek reconciliation. I had to make the first move.

Reconciliation is an act of restoring relationships and is crucial in the Christian life. Jesus said, 'So if you are standing before the altar in the Temple, offering a sacrifice to God, and suddenly remember that a friend has something against you, leave your sacrifice there beside the altar and go and apologize and be reconciled to him, and then come and offer your sacrifice to God' (Matthew 5:23–24, New Living Bible).

This journey was exceedingly difficult, but I knew I must take this step forward. My nature finds it easier to be reconciled to God than to contemplate reconciliation with people who are murderers. However, I had learned that Christ, who is the sinless Son of God, had come into this broken world in order to reconcile the world to himself. He had put himself in the position of being actually reconciled to sinners, without doing any harm or injury to his justice and holiness. Christ was willing to enter into a new treaty or a new covenant of grace whereby he freely forgave us all our sins.

Now the important part of this passage is that Christ gave us the ministry of reconciliation and we are his ambassadors. We need to free ourselves and to free those who offend us. As ambassadors of Christ, we are supposed to carry on his assignment of being reconciled with offenders. This goes against the natural mind of man, and many refuse to embrace it because it touches our pride. It is easy to direct other people to travel this road, but we have a hard time travelling it ourselves. To travel this way, one has to be willing to accept a second level of torment and hurt, but at the end of the road is a heart at peace. How could I go there? I had been deeply hurt and emotionally damaged by the killers. Going to see them in order to proclaim the message of mercy and reconciliation would not make sense to most people. It had taken me many years to think about such a trip, but as I prayed before leaving, I thought, 'Today, I will write a new script for my life – the living testimony of the grace of God in my life.'

Earlier, while at Tyndale University College in Canada, I had learned a lot about reconciliation from literature and from the professors, but I had never thought of meeting the killers. It is easy to give mental assent to things we learn from books or professors, and even to agree that it is morally right. However, putting it into practice is hard. It requires strong determination to accomplish this most difficult task. Such strong determination has to be born out of a character that reflects Christ's example. It is not enough merely to say, 'I forgive my family's killers'; rather, it has to come from my pure and sincere heart that really means to set the killers free from myself, and at the same time to free myself from them. I was once locked into death with the root of unforgiveness, which prevented me from communicating and being open with others. Now that I had removed the root of unforgiveness from within me, I could begin to build up my communication and openness to others again by being reconciled with the killers. Reconciliation is a fruit of real forgiveness. Forgiveness is not complete without it. This is how Christ demonstrates his forgiveness – through reconciliation. So I must follow his example if I want to grow in the faith and be an instrument in his plans and purposes. The time to go and accomplish this seemingly impossible task had now come. Although I was ready to undertake this mission, I knew that I would be hurt again, but for the sake of personal healing, I must bear the hurt and endure the second pain so that my soul, once drenched in agony and despair beyond words, would be fully restored to real life in Christ. I would know health, joy and a peace that passes all understanding. This peace would guard my thoughts and renew my tortured mind and give me strength to walk with God wherever he might direct me.

I also learned that the teaching of reconciliation given here is a crucial duty for each one of us. It is an absolute necessity, and it is not optional, if we are to be Christ's ambassadors. As God is willing to be reconciled to us, we ought to be reconciled to God. We are Christ's ambassadors, sent to treat sinners with peace and mercy. I knew that the purpose of my trip was to lay aside what they had done to my family and be reconciled to them with the love of Jesus Christ. My prayer on this trip was that reconciliation would become possible.

As I travelled to meet them, I stopped at my sister's house and told her what I was doing. She was shocked, so I asked her, 'Sister, how do you feel this morning, as I am about to make my trip to meet our family's killers and forgive them?'

She was unable to understand why I would do such a thing and was quite alarmed for my safety. She was speechless because she did not really understand what it meant to forgive killers, and I could tell that she was frightened of losing me. She feared that the killers would attempt to finish me off for good, and she was scared that I would lose control of my anger when I met them.

Reassuringly I told her, 'I feel peace this morning, after a long time of prayer. It has taken me more than twenty years to come to this point. I feel that God wants me to get my unfinished business done in a spiritual way. I will go with peace of mind and with the grace of God, and I will forgive them. I am an ambassador of Christ, and I will bring the message of forgiveness and reconciliation to the family's killers. It is morally right for me to do this. I know that you do not really understand what I am doing but, one day, you will understand this message.'

Before I left, I said a short prayer with her and gave her a hug. She said, 'May God protect you on your long journey and may God bless you.'

I left my house at 6.00 a.m. and collected Pastors Narath and Sokcheat, who were coming with me. I told them that I desperately needed their company for emotional and moral support. As we travelled together on one motorbike to Kokpreach village, we talked a lot. We all felt apprehensive about what lay ahead. How would we find the killers? I was not sure whether they were still alive, as I had left the village more than twenty years ago. Pastor Narath was silent. He is a very quiet man and, despite me trying to encourage him to talk, he just said, 'If I were you, I would not know what to do, and I would not have the guts to face those who had murdered my family. It is not easy, and I see it is a very painful decision, but I am very proud of you.' I was encouraged by his few words. He did not realize that inside my heart I was wrestling with uneasiness. He might think that I was a strong man, but the truth was that I was weak. I kept reciting my prayer that God would grant me strength to be able to accomplish this impossible mission.

I also respected what Pastor Narath had said because I knew that this visit did not make sense to him. Many people around me had been shocked to hear that I was going to make such a trip. They thought I was abnormal because no one in Cambodian society had ever done this. Some people thought I had been brainwashed by Christian teaching from the West; others asked me what my expectations were in meeting the family's killers. Whatever they said made sense to them, but I realized that they had never been exposed to the real teaching of forgiveness. Rather, they had been trained to forget the past and bury it. Accepting this teaching of forgiveness is difficult for Cambodians because they have not chosen this way. They do not know how to forgive because they are trying to forget about the past. I, too, thought like them before I became a Christian, and I still retained this philosophy for several years afterwards, but I had no peace or healing of my wounds. This day I was choosing to be released from the bondage of the past and to know healing of my wounds. I prayed that our nation might also seek forgiveness and know the healing of its wounds through the knowledge of Christ as Saviour and Lord.

I am a new person in Christ, and as such my role is that of his ambassador, and I am required to do something that reflects his character. People will not know that I am his ambassador unless I imitate my Lord's example. My old character is buried in the grave. I am now clothed with a Christian uniform – Christ's righteousness has been imputed to me because he has taken all my sins, particularly the sin of an unforgiving spirit. I have to live in accordance with this truth. Paul said, 'Do not conform any longer to the pattern of this world, but be transformed by the renewing of your mind' (Romans

12:2). I am no longer the person I once was, but a new person who is being transformed by the renewing of his mind. That new character has new sympathy, understanding, conscience, morals, spirit and purpose in life. I must live my life according to this new understanding, and these are the ingredients of a good ambassador. Whatever people said was not important, and what I was doing would not make sense to them, but I knew that my Lord would delight in seeing me try to accomplish this impossible mission.

As I write this, twenty-eight years have passed since the Khmer Rouge killed my family. At that time they were my enemies and I wanted their blood. I wanted them to suffer as I had suffered. Now, being an ambassador of Christ, I should never again be influenced by the pursuit of family honour. God's grace has transformed my life into a new creation in Christ, so I have to live accordingly. I had to choose to make my enemies my friends. Like me, they were broken Cambodians, and they needed to hear the message of the salvation and love of Jesus Christ just as much as I did. As I write these things, I wonder how many Christians in the West still hold an unforgiving spirit towards another Christian who has offended them in some small detail. If you do, it will hold up your relationship with Christ, and there is a serious teaching to bear in mind: 'if you do not forgive men their sins, your Father will not forgive your sins' (Matthew 6:15).

Paul said, 'Bear with each other and forgive whatever grievances you may have against one another. Forgive as the Lord forgave you. And over all these virtues put on love, which binds them all together in perfect unity' (Colossians 3:13–14). No matter how deep the hurt I had suffered, I had to face the killers, forgive them and love them. I believe that it is the love of Jesus Christ that has transformed me in order that the beauty of his forgiveness can be seen in my life. As I travelled, I knew that my mission was only one of forgiveness and reconciliation. It was proof of the greatness of God and the love of Jesus in my life. This proof has to be reflected in my character if I am to be God's ambassador.

Many friends in high-ranking positions had offered to send some of their soldiers with me, since there might be tension with the killers or threats from them. The village is a long way from the town and most of its residents were formerly Khmer Rouge soldiers, who were illiterate and generally ignorant, so my friends encouraged me to be careful with them. They thought I shouldn't risk going there without some protection. I told my friends that I did not need weapons and bodyguards, but I trusted the Lord. I prepared myself not with weapons but with the peace of Christ. 'Let the peace of Christ rule in your hearts, since as members of one body you were called to peace. And be thankful' (Colossians 3:15). If I were to bring soldiers with me, the people in the village would never believe that I had come to bring the message of forgiveness. They would interpret my return to the village as an attempt to settle the score for my family. It would bring another form of confusion to the people in the village. I realized that it was a big risk for my life. It was very uncertain, but I should not need soldiers to go with me. All I needed was the grace of God. I allowed my uncertainty to be ruled by the peace of God rather than weapons and soldiers.

The road to the village was in very poor condition: in fact it was little more than a track for ox-carts. My bones ached from jolting along the countless bumps, but I had to endure this discomfort because the trip was a component of my new life in Christ. Even though it caused me physical and mental pain, I must pursue it in obedience to Christ. An hour before we reached the village, we stopped, rested and prayed for the peace of the Lord. I told Pastors Sokcheat and Narath that my eldest brother had been killed not far from the place where we were resting. I felt the great loss of my older brothers again; my lips and tongue felt numb as painful memories began to rise. Pastors Sokcheat and Narath noticed the sudden change in my face and recognized that I felt uneasy. As we neared the village, I relived many painful memories, but I thanked God that I could retrieve all of these memories and lay them at the foot of the cross. As I began that process, I started sharing with the two pastors what my life in the village had been like. Twenty years earlier, I could never have dreamed of returning to this village, and if I had returned, I would have come with soldiers to wipe out the village and everyone living in it, in order to extinguish my anger. I thanked God for sparing my life, and for the pathway he had chosen for me to walk, to give me the needed strength and grace to bring his message of forgiveness through Jesus Christ to these killers.

Pastors Sokcheat and Narath were moved by my experiences, but even they did not really understand my motivation for coming to meet the killers. I had tried to explain to them about the Christian life – that we should learn to forgive our enemies – but they were young in their faith, as I had once been, so they had difficulty in understanding what I was trying to do. They had heard messages about forgiveness and had learned from the

Bible, but putting those lessons into personal practice is not always as easy as hearing or reading about them. They did not ask any questions; instead they listened intently.

As I was about to enter the village, the sharpness of my painful memories intensified. So I prayed silently, 'Lord, I feel uneasy approaching this village. The unwanted emotional legacies are stirring within me. Please help me to handle these in a healthy way and with a Christian character that reflects yours. I need your guidance, Lord, and I need to be a good ambassador. Please show me your grace and give me strength to face the most difficult task in my life. I am only human. I feel hurt and pain, but I know that you are going with me. Please help me to accomplish this almost impossible mission of forgiveness. Lord, such forgiveness is proof of your greatness and your love in my life. Help me to do what is morally right and help me to know what to say to them. I know that it will be difficult, but help me not to rely on my own strength and wisdom. Help me to rely on your strength and grace. Help me to behave as your ambassador. Be with me, Lord. I need your help. I need you to guide me to behave in an appropriate way which will reflect your character of forgiveness. Lord God, I ask you to be with me.'

Pastors Sokcheat and Narath were aware that I was trying to pray, but they felt inadequate and just wanted to accompany me as my supporters. We were now nearing the village and I could feel my heart pounding with fear. From time to time, I tried to take deep breaths to ease the tension.

Pastor Narath noticed my uneasiness and said, 'How do you feel now?'

'I'm feeling a bit uneasy, but I think I can deal with it as I entrust this trip to the Lord,' I responded.

He smiled and commented, 'I would not see myself coming to meet my family's killers, like you.'

I just said, 'Thank you for your honesty. As you know, I would never have dreamed of coming back to the village to meet my family's killers, but I feel as though I have some unfinished business here. I need a new start in my life, so I am choosing forgiveness by letting go of all the pains and hurts of the past, and I am choosing to receive healing for my wounds. I know that God has spared my life and taken me back to this village for just this special purpose. He has a special assignment for me to accomplish.'

Pastor Narath didn't know what to say to me, and I wasn't sure he understood me, because he was speechless and made no attempt to interact with me. I sensed that he had captured something of my intentions but had no idea how I felt deep inside. I felt as though the Lord had spoken to me through the words of Philippians 3:13–14: 'Forgetting what is behind and straining towards what is ahead, I press on towards the goal to win the prize for which God has called me heavenwards in Christ Jesus.'

In my heart and in God's eyes, I had already forgiven them, but coming to face them was another matter. Pain and fear accompanied me on this journey, yet come what may, I was determined to face them. I felt I would not be upset if they did not seek my forgiveness. My duty was only to obey God, even though they had wronged me. I should expect nothing from them. I knew that it was an extraordinary journey for me. I must not allow any internal emotion to hinder my journey.

With these words of encouragement from the Bible, I was able to press on towards completing the task and to overcome the fear and pain I had experienced so many years ago. 'I can do everything through him who gives me strength' (Philippians 4:13). I had taken much time to come to this place of forgiveness through the patient, loving compassion and grace of God. I must no longer hold onto the emotional legacies that had crippled both my life and my relationship with God – I had to let it all go.

As I meditated on this passage, God spoke to me: 'Trust in me. I will take you through this journey. My peace will rule your life. I have taken you on a long journey – I will take you a few extra miles. All you need to do is trust in me. I am your Good Shepherd.'

This reminded me of Psalm 23:1–4:

The Lord is my shepherd, I shall not be in want.
He makes me lie down in green pastures,
he leads me beside quiet waters,
he restores my soul.
He guides me in paths of righteousness
for his name's sake.
Even though I walk
through the valley of the shadow of death,
I will fear no evil,
for you are with me;
your rod and your staff,
they comfort me.

As I reflected on this psalm, I felt secure in God's righteousness. I knew he was with me. I felt safe because I knew that he is my Good Shepherd.

By 10 a.m. we arrived in the village and I went to look

for my foster-father. He was still alive but was not at home that day. My foster-mother was there, and it was an enormous surprise for her to see me. Word soon went round the village and a number of the folk came to see me at my foster-parents' house. They were all surprised by my return to the village where I had lost my family. There were many I didn't recognize, so I introduced myself to them. Not many of the villagers knew me, because most of my generation had been killed during the long civil war.

I asked about those who had been involved in killing my family. They were shocked at such a question. Why had I come back to look for the family's killers? I had been missing for more than twenty years, and now, unexpectedly, I was back in the village asking about the murderers of my family. What was my motivation? I sensed that they were thinking that I had come to take revenge. At first, they did not tell me where the killers were, and I could tell that some of them were very frightened. They did not look happy and some were very nervous. A few people tried to comfort me and persuade me to forget what had happened in the past. They said, 'We had no desire to kill your family but we were forced to do so. If we had not obeyed the higher organization, we would have been killed ourselves. We were left with no choice.'

I could tell that they were feeling guilty. They were trying to make reasonable excuses and pretended they were good people. Many of the younger generation, who had heard of my story, came to look at me. Suddenly, they started talking about me – how I had survived the execution and had disappeared for so many years. Some older people also came to see me, but they could not recognize me at all. I could tell that they were afraid of me, especially those who were related to my family's killers.

I had been right: if I had come with weapons and soldiers, the people in this village would have been scared of me. No one would have trusted me. They might have run away from me. I had a hard time building up my initial trust-relationship with them. I could tell that they were not feeling secure. They were so suspicious about me. No one who had lost his family had ever come back to look for their killers and to offer forgiveness. If they were to come back, they would do so in order to settle the score.

Pastors Sokcheat and Narath told me that the people were afraid of me. They thought I had come back to take revenge for my family. That was why they were so distant from me. They did not trust me. Many people were asking Pastors Sokcheat and Narath why I had come.

I said to the people in the village, 'My desire in coming here today is to meet those people who were involved in killing my family and to forgive them. I do not intend to do anything harmful to them, but I just want to tell them that I have come to cancel what I actually wanted to do to them more than twenty years ago.' After I had made this statement, the people were even more perplexed.

Pastors Narath and Sokcheat reinforced my message: 'He is a Christian, he does not believe in killing. He just wants to meet those people who were involved in killing his family and to forgive them. Please do not fear. He will not hurt anybody.' They were trying so hard to pass on the message of forgiveness, but the people found the idea hard to understand. And when they heard the new word 'Christian', this created yet more confusion for them. They had no idea of what a Christian believes and does. It was the first time they had heard about Christian people.

Pastor Sokcheat tried to explain: 'Christians are people who believe in Jesus Christ, the Son of God who came to this world to die for the sin of all human beings. People who believe in Jesus Christ are called Christians. They do not believe in killing. Reaksa is a Christian. He does not believe in killing, but believes in forgiving. He has come here today to meet those who were involved in killing his family and to offer his forgiveness to them. So you should not be afraid of him. He will not do anything harmful to anyone here. Please do not feel afraid. He comes here to bring peace, not killing.'

For a little while, I could perceive a mood shift in some of them, showing appreciation. However, other people were still sceptical about my motives. It did not make sense to them and it was unthinkable that anyone would ever come to search for their family's killers and forgive them.

No one would tell me where the killers were, so I had no idea who had survived the long, intense civil war or where they were. I went to look for my old friend Sak, with whom I used to work in the fields during the Khmer Rouge period. He had become blind since we had last met, but although he could not see me, he instantly recognized my voice. He had been forced to join the Khmer Rouge soldiers, who ordered him and his two friends to catch fish by using bombs. One of his friends made a mistake, and a bomb killed both of them. Sak was blinded and almost lost his life. I spent some time with him and told him of my desire to return to the village. He and his family live in the same area where my family lived during the Khmer Rouge regime. While speaking to Sak's family, I recalled the painful memory of my younger brother's torture in front of my mother. She had wanted to cry, but in front of the evil *chlops*, she had suppressed her feelings for fear of being executed. I also recalled the painful moment when my father had been arrested by the *chlops*. I had called my younger brothers and sister and had told them, 'They arrested our father, and I think they are going to kill us today.' This phrase started echoing in my ears. I remembered trying to embrace my younger brothers and sister, but we were all trembling uncontrollably.

I spoke to God in silence: 'Father God in heaven, I can feel all the pain in my heart. Being back in this painful place intensifies my inner emotions. I can remember all the things that happened to my family many years ago. However, I thank you for sparing my life from the grave and for bringing me back to this place. It is not easy for me to be back. Please comfort my heart and grant me peace of mind to deal with this painful moment in my life.'

Sak's mother asked me, 'Do you remember this place? This is the place where your family used to live. How do you feel now?'

I responded, 'Yes, I remember this place and all that happened to my family, and I feel broken-hearted that I shall never see any of them again.'

My honest response stunned her a bit. She didn't ask any more questions. She was afraid that her questions would hurt my feelings.

After a long conversation with my friend Sak, I told his family, 'I would like to tell you one thing. My parents buried some gold and two diamond rings from the gifts they got at their wedding. I cannot recall the exact spot where they buried them, but you may try to look for them.'

Sak was very helpful to me and said that four of the six killers had been killed during the Vietnamese invasion; only two men had survived and one of them had moved out to live in a neighbouring village. I knew the two survivors: Ean was the one who had moved, while Mao still lived in the village. So I went to his house, but he wasn't there. He was working in the fields, so I asked Pastor Sokcheat and a village man to go and look for him and bring him to my foster-father's house so that we could talk together. I sent a short message with Pastor Sokcheat: 'Please tell him not to worry, as my intentions are good; I just want to meet him and forgive him.' I also said the same thing to the man who accompanied Pastor Sokcheat; I wanted to reassure him that I had no evil intent to hurt Mao. They left to look for him.

While waiting for Mao to come, I spoke to a number of people in the village and learned which men in my generation had been killed during the civil war. Many older people were still alive but they seemed to have forgotten what had happened to my family. At first they were afraid of speaking to me but, eventually, they felt comfortable enough to ask me where I had been for the last twenty-five years or so. I met an older woman who had provoked the 'old liberated people' to destroy my eldest brother Sophoan. The moment I saw her, I recalled every word she had said when my eldest brother had been falsely accused of stealing rice. Her words flooded my mind: 'Destroy him! Destroy him! He is the *khmang* of the *angkar loeu*. Don't keep him!' During that time she had been an evil woman, but when I met her again, there was no trace of remorse or regret for the past. I humbled myself to speak politely to her, as I didn't want to do anything that would remind her of our meeting so many years ago. I gave her some medicines and clothes for her family as a blessing. I said in my heart, 'God, this woman does not even remember or show any remorse for what she did to my family. Forgive her, Lord. Please help me not to hold any bitterness or anger against her.'

Mao was ploughing his rice paddy when Pastor Sokcheat approached him and told him of my visit. He was shocked to hear that I had invited him to come and see me in the village. Mao thought that I had disappeared twenty years ago, so he was amazed that I had returned to meet him. He didn't know what my motivation was for the meeting, but he stopped his ploughing, left his cows to eat in the field and came back to the village. Before his arrival in the village, Pastor Sokcheat tried to explain that I would like to meet him and forgive him. He did not have a clue about forgiveness. He was thinking that I would come to take revenge for my family. Pastor Sokcheat also told him, 'You do not need to fear Reaksa. He has no intention to hurt you or kill you, but he comes here to forgive you.' Mao was speechless. He did not know what to say to Pastor Sokcheat. He seemed so suspicious about what Pastor Sokcheat had said to him; it did not seem to make any sense to him at all. He was filled with fear and insecurity.

When he arrived, I could see he was putting on a good exterior face, but underneath he was fearful, so I approached him and greeted him. He tried to smile but couldn't speak, so I invited him to sit down and have lunch with me. Several other people joined us for lunch, and as I had brought some bread from home, I gave Mao some as I sat beside him, trying to make him feel at ease. While he tried to regain his composure, someone offered him some alcohol while he was having lunch with us. He drank a little and began to talk to me. After finishing lunch, I took the initiative and asked him how he felt about meeting me. He did not answer but just smiled. He had killed my father and had hit me, so I asked him, 'Do you know where you hit me?'

He responded, 'Yes, I do.'

I asked him, 'Did you know how many people you killed that day?'

He said, 'No, I don't remember.'

I said, 'There were thirty-three people, but only thirty-two died. I am the sole survivor.'

I could tell that he was surprised but he said nothing. He could not figure out what was my motivation to meet him. As I asked him about how he had hit me and how many people he and his associates had killed on that day, I could tell that fear had crept into his heart. He looked so frightened. He was so nervous to face me. He could not look at my eyes.

'Let me tell you about my mission today,' I said to him. 'I have come here to set you free from the bondage of fear. I have brought gifts for you. Here is a *krama*' (a Cambodian scarf). I put it on his shoulder and said, 'This *krama* is a symbol of my forgiveness for you. Here is my shirt I have brought for you as a symbol of my love for you.'

Then I gave him a Khmer New Testament as a symbol of my blessing for him. I opened it at Matthew 23:34: 'Father, forgive them, for they do not know what they are doing.' I read this passage out loud and said, 'I have come here today to cancel in person what I vowed to do for my family more than twenty-five years ago, which was to take revenge. My mission in coming here is, by the grace of God, to forgive what you did to my family.'

I asked him, 'Do you know how to read?'

'No, I don't know how to read,' he replied, 'but I can ask my children to read it for me.'

I was encouraged by his positive response. It was a moment of emotional deliverance for me to preach the message of forgiveness to the man who had killed my father. Years before, I would not have been able to believe that I could one day deliver that message. It was the grace of God that enabled me to say, 'I forgive you.'

Even though I had been determined to offer forgiveness, I found it very difficult to get the words out as I stood before the man who had killed my father. My throat choked with unspoken words and my heart ached with pain. I was convinced that the Holy Spirit was touching my heart to heal the wounds of unforgiveness. Without question, I had forgiven the killers, but the wound inflicted by the root of unforgiveness was still raw. It had not been healed completely, because throughout the years of learning about forgiveness, I knew that it centred on enduring the second suffering. Real forgiveness arises from the ability to endure this pain. The first hurt had become part of my life, whereas I had consciously embraced the wound from the root of unforgiveness. Now it was hard to open it again for the final healing. Facing the family's killers enabled the Holy Spirit to touch my heart in a new way and bring about healing. If you have a wound in your leg, you remove the plaster and cleanse the wound. It stings, but healing is taking place. Cleansing the wound is necessary for the healing process. Facing the family's killer and offering forgiveness to him brought healing to my wounded soul. Delivering the message of forgiveness to the man who had killed my father opened my heart for healing. It was extremely painful to say, 'I forgive you', but it brought healing.

The hurt was tremendously deep, but it was, in a sense, the means of being liberated from the bondage of bitterness. I thanked God for granting me the courage and ability to endure the second suffering through which genuine forgiveness was produced. I knew I was now liberated from the wounds of bitterness. I removed the image of the killers from my head and no longer embraced bitterness. After delivering my message of forgiveness to him, I realized that Mao did not really understand what I meant by the grace of God. I felt as though I was trying to pour water on a duck's head and he hadn't the ability to absorb my message of forgiveness because he was afraid of me. I consoled him and told him not to be afraid any more, and he acknowledged that he was not afraid of me. But when I put my right arm on his shoulder, I could feel his body trembling. I could tell that he felt as I had once felt when he had taken my family into the jungle for execution. He pretended to be brave but, inside, he was frightened and insecure.

I tried to ask him questions about his feelings, but he showed no emotion, no regret and no remorse over what he had done to my family. He seemed dead inside. The devil's spirit controlled his emotions so that he had no feelings. I asked him, 'How do you feel now that I have said I have forgiven you?'

His response was 'Thank you.'

After spending three hours with him, I gave Mao a hug and said, 'By the grace of God, I can forgive you. I know that you did not intend to kill my family but it was done under orders from the Khmer Rouge. What happened in the past is now, by the grace of God, cancelled and you may go in peace. May God bless you. May the spirit of fear subside from you.'

Inside my heart, I was crying. I could feel the pain of delivering these words to the man who had actually killed my family, but I thank God for granting me the courage to deliver such words. Mao said nothing but he smiled at me. During my time spent with him, I only wished I could have heard him say, 'I am so sorry for what happened to your family.' He showed no sign of regret or remorse, but perhaps he didn't know how to express his emotions. Neither had he ever experienced forgiveness before, so he didn't know how to accept it from me. Disregarding his response, in my heart I knew that I had done my part and that God was happy with my mission. I felt I could hear him say, 'Well done, Reaksa. You have obeyed my word. Your conduct has reflected my Son's character.'

Many people in the village were stunned to see me giving my family's killer a hug. It is very uncommon in Cambodian culture to see men hugging. It only happens if the two men have been extremely close to each other for many years, and are meeting again or saying farewell. I had hugged the man who had killed my family, and it didn't make sense to the village people. They were suspicious of my actions and probably thought my behaviour was just an act – I was just putting on a good show. They were afraid that I might come back one day to finish Mao off.

The former deputy village leader who had received the order from the *angkar loeu* and had given the final order to Mao and his associates to kill my family, passed by, so I called him over to have a chat. He was the authority behind the killing, so I asked him to stop a little while because I had an important message for him. He was also shocked at seeing me, having been told of my disappearance over twenty-five years earlier. Now, here I was, back in the village where my family had died. In his astonishment, he too thought I had come with bad intentions. He was speechless and very nervous, and he heard people who were standing with us say, 'He was the deputy village leader then, and he made all the decisions, good or bad.' Other people said, 'He was the one who gave the orders to kill your family.'

He was very frightened already, and these extra statements created a deeper fear within him – so much so that he appeared to have a problem with breathing. He began to respond to what the people were saying and shouted, 'I didn't want to do it but I was forced to! What could I do?' His words silenced the crowd; they knew that what he said was true. He was trying to defend his moral ethic. I did not intend to pressure him. I just wanted to have a short talk with him and tell him that I forgave him.

I bowed down and greeted him, and he did the same to me. As I came closer to him, putting my hand on his shoulder, I could hear his stressed breathing.

'What is wrong with you?' I asked kindly.

He replied: 'I can hardly breathe.'

I could see that his body was trembling uncontrollably. He was like a baby chick in my hand, so I tried to calm him down. 'My mission today is to set you free from the debt you owe my family. I have come not to do anything harmful to you, but rather, to forgive you. I have already forgiven Mao.' I pointed to Mao.

As soon as he heard the message of forgiveness and looked at Mao, he relaxed. I took a Cambodian scarf and put it around his neck and said, 'This is my symbol of forgiveness, and it cancels all the evil you did to my family. You may go in peace, and may God bless you.'

He said nothing and I knew he didn't really understand what I meant by forgiveness. I spent a little longer with him, chatting about his life, and he asked about my life after I had left the village. I told him some of the appalling difficulties I had faced, but he showed no sign of pity or remorse. I knew he had been ordered to kill my family, but at least he could have shown some remorse.

During our conversation he told me he was very sick. He had stomach-aches and fever in the night and was gradually losing weight; he coughed a lot at night and had difficulty with breathing. I gave him some medication to help him with his stomach-ache and suggested that he should be tested for TB. I asked him to come to the city to get a chest X-ray and assured him I was willing to help him. He said he did not have enough money to make the trip to the city, so I offered to cover the cost of his trip there and back. He thought for a while, and finally, he said that he would come.

I tried to find the second deputy village leader, who had also been involved in making the decision to kill my family. People in the village told me that the man had become psychologically crippled. He didn't know anyone and seemed unable to know who he was. People advised me not to go near him, as he was not stable psychologically. Whenever he saw a stranger, he would scream and run away from home. Day by day he talked to himself and neglected his clothes and personal hygiene. I was reminded of the day of my family's execution; he and his associates had dug the grave for them. I took the advice of the village folk and didn't go to see him, but I left a message of forgiveness with them to pass on to him, if they thought he could hear it.

Before leaving the village, I promised the people I would come back to help with wells and a school. I also shared with them that what I had been able to do that day was not done in my own strength but by the grace of God. This same God had saved me from the grave because he had a special purpose for my life. He wanted me to bring them the message of hope, love and salvation through the gift of forgiveness we receive when we come into a relationship with Jesus Christ, the Saviour of the world.

I left word with the village people that I would like to meet the other surviving killer, Ean, and forgive him. He was my mother's killer. I told them I would like to come back again the following month to meet him.

I felt that this day had achieved a lot. I had been able to speak to these men whom, formerly, I would have been only too glad to kill. Forgiving had released me from those harmful thoughts, but I was drained emotionally and glad to start the journey home with Pastors Sokcheat and Narath.

On our way home, I was unable to talk to Pastor Sokcheat because he was driving the motorbike; Pastor Narath sat in the middle and I was on the back seat. I spoke to Pastor Narath about the day's events, and he still could hardly believe that I had been able to return to meet the family's killers and the people in the village where I had once been so deeply hurt.

A few weeks afterwards, Pastor Narath came to me with a confession: 'I learned many things from you, particularly how you forgave your family's killers. One thing I could not accept was that you were able to hug the man who killed your father. It actually hurt me to watch you doing that.' When I asked him what made him feel that way, his response was, 'Because I couldn't do what you've done; it is so hard, and painful too. If I were in your shoes, I couldn't do it.'

I was silent, because I had no idea how to respond. In reality, it had not been an easy lesson for me, and it had taken years for me to learn to forgive. But I was glad that Pastor Narath was able to be honest with me. It was an acknowledgment that such a thing is not as easy as many preachers think. It is true that forgiveness is difficult to practise for some Christians who have been hurt gravely, but others who have had an untroubled life and very few traumas find it easy.

Recently I spoke to a group of American short-term missionaries who had come to do medical check-ups in my house churches. One member of this group – a former American soldier in the Vietnam War – stood up after hearing my story of forgiveness and said, 'I have been a Christian for sixty-two years. If I were you, I would kill them. I would shoot one bullet into his body and put another in his head.'

I was shocked to hear this, but I could appreciate his honesty. I realized that forgiveness is not easy to accomplish. I responded, 'Thank you for your honesty. It has taken me many years to work through this painful process, but I thank God for granting me strength to work through it and forgive.'

He asked me to speak at his church in California one day, then added, 'American people need to hear your message of forgiveness. It would help them to heal their hurt.'

A few weeks after my trip to meet the killers, my church-planting partner wrote to me:

Dear Reaksa

When I first read your life story, I felt sad and angry. I was sad to read of the evil done to you and your family and I was angry that the wicked seem to triumph. Yet towards the end of this narrative, you shared about the peace and freedom God granted to you to forgive these evil men. I was very touched – both by your willingness to forgive and your honest admission of your struggle to forgive. But most of all I was overwhelmed by the incredible miracle that God has wrought in your heart. However, all these emotions and thoughts remained outside the realm of my personal life. They were real, no doubt, but yet far from the reality of my day-to-day existence. Then God granted me this tremendous privilege of working with you in partnership to serve him in Cambodia. Suddenly the words, the thoughts and the emotions took on flesh and bones. Working with you, hearing you share about your plans to bless the Cambodians and watching you minister to a people that once hurt you so deeply has made me feel ashamed of my own inability to forgive. It has not been easy working by your side. Why? Because your life exposed the great gulf between beliefs and practice that exists in my own life. I asked myself, 'Would I be able to forgive the killers of my entire family?' I found myself weak and lacking in this area. Somebody once said, 'The weak can never forgive. Forgiveness is the attitude of the strong.' Reaksa, you are the strong one and I thank God for the strength he has put in you. Surely it takes divine love and strength to not only forgive but to seek to meet the killers one by one so that you could tell them face to face that you forgive them and to bless them with gifts. Truly this is repaying evil with good. Truly this is the gospel of Jesus Christ clothed with

flesh and blood! It is my prayer that the Lord will continue
to use you to proclaim the message of forgiveness and reconciliation – a message that the world needs to hear and
the church needs to recover. May the Lord bless you richly.

Your friend

Pak Soon Lau

*   *   *

The weak can never forgive. Forgiveness is the attitude of
the strong.   *Arthur D. Ficke*

Forgiveness is a choice – a step-by-step process.
                                        Robert D. Enright

*   *   *

A month after my trip to the village, I asked Pastor
Sokcheat to go back there to see if he could find Ean; he
did, and persuaded him to meet me. Pastor Sokcheat
also met Mao again, and Mao told him that he had not
been able to sleep for weeks after I had left. Mao was
afraid that, because I had taken some pictures of him, I
would send someone to kill him. He had been so terrified
after seeing me that he had convinced himself that I was
going to kill him sooner rather than later.

Pastor Sokcheat tried to reassure him: 'Reaksa is a
Christian. He would not come to take your life. He does
not believe in killing because God does not allow us to
kill other people. Please do not worry so much. Rather,
you should open your heart to accept Jesus Christ as your
Lord and Saviour.'

Mao did not know how to read and it was hard for

Sokcheat to motivate him to read the Bible that I had given him, so Sokcheat took some time to share with him about the Christian faith and about Jesus Christ, who came into the world to bring people to God. He had no concept of the Christian faith. His only perception was that Jesus Christ is the foreigners' God.

Pastor Sokcheat and I made a second trip to meet Ean, but it was disappointing because he had gone to work in the fields. Two people from the village went to look for him and sent a message asking him to come and see me in the town, as I would pay all his expenses. I returned home deeply disappointed because there was no reply. I tried to look for the former second deputy village leader, but again the village people tried to persuade me that it would be a waste of time seeing him.

When I eventually made my third trip to search for Ean, I woke up very early in the morning and went to collect Pastors Vansan and Sokcheat to go with me. Pastor Vansan had studied at the Phnom Penh Bible School before joining my group of house churches.

Before we reached the village, we stopped for a prayer time, asking the Lord for direction and help in meeting Ean. Pastor Vansan, being new to the area, didn't know about my family background, so I told him about it, and he was sad and remained quiet for a while. Then he prayed for my meeting with Ean.

When we reached the village, again Ean was not there, and I was told he was in another village called Rok. His friend told me, 'Ean has an appointment with me today. He is supposed to be here by now but has not shown up yet. Wait for a little while; he will be here soon.'

We waited two hours, and during that time I met two other men who had harmed my family. Seeth had accused my brother Sophoan of stealing his two cans of rice and had been instrumental in his brutal torture. I could picture my brother with his arms tied backwards to the post and the mosquitoes biting him throughout the whole night. I never forgot an earlier night, when Seeth had stood up and said, 'We don't like to have the *khmang* of the *angkar loeu* living among us. We have to destroy them. We need to separate them from us clearly. Do you know the *khmang* among us? He is with Sophoan.' Those words said many years ago and the fear they had caused me seemed to reverberate in my ears. The cruelty inflicted on my brother was so inhumane, especially as he had done nothing to deserve it. When he was released he was sent to work in another village, and that was the last time I ever saw him.

Now I approached Seeth and greeted him and, to my amazement, he had no memory of what he had done. He may have remembered what he had done to my family, but perhaps the devil's spirit controlled his life so completely that it crippled his emotions, making him dead inside. Maybe he had suppressed his own conscience so much that he could no longer feel regret or remorse. A person like this, living with a dead conscience, cannot wake up to life on his own. Maybe he, like the apostle Paul, needed a wake-up call from the Holy Spirit.

I did not say much to Seeth, and he realized that I was not too interested in listening to him. He turned to speak to Pastors Sokcheat and Vansan, pretending to be a good man, and telling them some fabricated stories of good deeds he had done. I could hear everything he said: 'Reaksa does not even remember that I am the one who helped him to stay alive. After his family was killed, he survived and came back to the village. That night, the

people in the village held a meeting and decided to finish him off, but I begged them not to kill him.' He
stopped after a little while and looked at me, but I said
nothing to him.

I knew he was not speaking the truth, but my mission
to this village was to forgive the people, not to bring up
more accusations. What he had said was a lie. I could still
vividly bring to mind his words that night: 'If you dig the
grass, you need to dig its roots too, or the grass will come
back again.' He had tried to persuade the people to finish me off! I wanted to confront him when I heard him
telling such an untrue story, but I kept remembering
that my mission was to forgive these people. I had to
remind myself not to expect any good things from them.
I felt as though the Spirit of God was reminding me that
I needed to forgive him, even though he would not
acknowledge his guilt. I chose not to confront him but
found a way to bring the conversation to a close.

After I had left him, I told Pastors Sokcheat and
Vansan, 'He wanted to end my life. Now, he pretends to
have said good things about me. If I were not a Christian,
and my mission were not to forgive these people, I would
break his neck in a few minutes.' I was very disturbed by
what he had said, but I had to manage my emotions and
calm down. 'God, please forgive this man. He does not
even know what he did to my family,' I prayed quietly,
but Pastors Sokcheat and Vansan were angry that my
efforts to bring forgiveness had met with such a rebut-
tal. It is easier to forgive the one who admits his mistakes than to forgive one who never admits his
wrongdoing. It was hard to forgive this man, but I knew
I must not let the root of unforgiveness control my life
again. I dared not embrace bitterness, despite the way he

had reacted to me. I must not hold onto what he had said; I must forgive. I prayed with Pastors Sokcheat and Vansan, 'Jesus, my Lord, forgive this man. Father God, I choose not to hook myself onto the bitterness, rage and hatred. Instead I choose to free myself from the bondage of these negative emotions and hurts. Holy Spirit, help me to let this man go free from me.'

The message of loving our enemies reminded me of what I should do to him. I remembered that Jesus said, 'Love your enemies, do good to those who hate you, bless those who curse you, pray for those who ill-treat you' (Luke 6:27–28). I came to realize that in order to love my family's killers, I had to first forgive them. This is a difficult and painful love, but I must follow my Master.

The second man I met, called Sal, had wrongly accused my younger brother of stealing two pieces of corn. He had brutally tortured my brother until he lost consciousness twice. I recalled how my brother's arms had been tied behind his back as he was led past our house; how he was then hung on our fence so that we could see them punish him. I shuddered at the memory. Sal and Mao had ordered us to watch them torturing my brother. To observe such an atrocity made me suffer beyond words. My brother was only ten years old; he was so badly beaten up that I couldn't recognize his face. We were powerless to stop them and watched helplessly, unable to speak or cry, while he hung on the fence and received the worst beating of his life. Now, Sal did not even remember what he had done to my brother. I wanted to confront him about what he had done, but then I decided not to do so, for I could not think of what I would gain from him if I did.

I asked myself why evil people never remember what they have done. This subject has taken up much of my time, and I have no answer for it. I knew I must hold to my ultimate mission – I had come to this village with the grace of God to forgive the wrongdoers. Placing a Cambodian scarf round his neck as a symbol of my forgiveness made no difference to his attitude. He did not repent of what he had done to my younger brother, but at least he didn't fabricate a story to give the impression that he was a good man. I didn't have such a hard time forgiving this man. 'Whatever happened in the past is now cancelled today,' I said to him. 'May the peace of Christ be with you and may God bless you.' He said nothing to me because he had no idea of the meaning of forgiveness. He did not really understand what I said about the grace of God. I believe that he didn't care to remember what he had done to my brother.

When Ean had not yet shown up after two hours, I decided to go to Rok village. I was determined to search for him and forgive him. There is only a rough track to Rok, so we had to ride the motorbike through dried rice-fields. This was bad for my back, but I had to endure this painful ride. When we finally arrived we looked for Ean's house, and his wife told us that he had just left for Kokpreach village. She was shocked to see me and asked Pastor Sokcheat, 'Is this the man who wanted to meet my husband last time?' Pastor Sokcheat responded, 'Yes, he is the man.' Her mood suddenly changed and her voice began to choke. She didn't know what to say to me, so I spoke to her and her two sons: 'I have come to forgive your husband. Do not worry that I will harm him. Here, I have brought some clothes and medicines for him. I desperately need to meet him to forgive him. I have been in Kokpreach village, but I could not find him. Please tell me the truth. Where is he?' She didn't really trust me, but Pastor Sokcheat helped to reassure her of my mission: 'He comes to bring peace for your family. Don't be afraid of him. He is a Christian; he doesn't believe in killing.' I could see the hint of a smile on her face, and she had told the truth when she had said that her husband had gone to Kokpreach village. I told Pastors Sokcheat and Vansan that we must not return home yet. Rather, we definitely needed to look for him in Kokpreach village before we went home.

On our arrival, Ean was waiting for me, so I thanked God for enabling me to fulfil my mission. He was so amazed to see me, although he did not fully recognize me. I had a long conversation with him. In contrast to the others, Ean acknowledged his guilt:

'I feel absolute regret for all I did. Indeed, I was forced to do things that have made me feel guilty for the rest of my life. You have to understand that I had no choice, because if I had disobeyed orders, I too would have been killed. But, no matter why I did it, it was wrong.'

I felt moved by what he said and delivered my message to him: 'I have come today to forgive you.'

He responded bravely: 'I would like to thank you so much that you are able to do this. Please forgive me the terrible wrong I did to your family.'

As soon as I heard these words, my heart wept. I was deeply touched, and I felt as though the pain from the burning fire of unforgiveness, which had previously been quenched, now brought about healing and restored my inner joy. This was the ultimate message, the one I had longed to hear all my life. He was the first among the killers to admit to what he had done and to ask for forgiveness.

He said, 'I heard you had returned to the village on

two occasions, but I missed seeing you. I did receive your
message, asking me to visit you, but my wife was afraid
you had come to take revenge. I thought about running
away, but then realized that there was nowhere to run to.
If you had wanted to kill me in retribution, I was ready
to face the consequences of all I did. I had no way of
escape, because even if I could run from you, I could
never run from the terrible guilt that has plagued my
life.'

I deliberately interrupted him: 'We are Christians. We
do not believe in killing, we believe in bringing the message of love, forgiveness and salvation to people. If I was
not a Christian, I would not have come to be reconciled
with you. Instead, I would have sent a few people to settle the score. Our God is full of compassion. He teaches
us to love, not to hate; to forgive, and never to kill. We
obey his teaching, and it is the power of his love that
melts the hatred inside my soul. That is why I have come
to face you and forgive you. Otherwise, I would have
taken revenge. But I thank God that we have met today.
I feel that I have completed my task.'

He replied, 'Your God is good. You are highly educated
and you understand what to do and how to forgive. Can
you tell me more about your God?'

In response, I said, 'I will. But let me ask you first,
how did you feel when you took our family to be executed?'

He looked very nervous, but took courage and said: 'I
was so frightened.'

I immediately confronted him: 'You say that you were
frightened, but why did you laugh when you killed people?'

He replied sadly, 'I didn't know what I was doing that

day, as far as I remember. I felt as though something was controlling my life. It was a kind of madness. During the first few killings, we were scared, but after that we felt that an evil spirit possessed us. We did not even know why we were doing it. We lost our humanity and were like monsters. Our madness led us to such unspeakable acts.'

While telling me his story – how he had killed my family – he looked deeply distressed and was aware of his guilt, showing both remorse and regret. My heart was overwhelmed when I heard that confession. He was so brave to speak to me as he had and to be honest. I was not sure why I had confronted him and why I had wanted to know what he had felt, but I now realized that I had taken him too far – in fact, beyond what I had intended to ask.

I was aware of Paul's warning in Ephesians 4:29: 'Do not let any unwholesome talk come out of your mouths, but only what is helpful for building others up according to their needs, that it may benefit those who listen.' If I kept pushing him to tell me more about what had happened to my family and how he had killed them, I could tell that evil things might come out of my mouth. I would accuse him or condemn him for the crime he had done.

For the sake of reconciliation, I chose to stop the confrontation. My purpose was to learn to love my family's killer and to forgive him. I had come to bring peace to him, not to make war. Jesus said, 'Blessed are the peacemakers, for they will be called sons of God' (Matthew 5:9). I believe that God was pleased with me for coming to make peace with my family's killers.

Finally I said to Ean, 'Let us cancel all the past and begin a new life. The past has been painfully written in my soul, but we need to begin afresh with the joy of life. Let me assure you once again that I have no evil desire to hurt you or your family. Rather, I have forgiven you. You do not need to worry about me coming to kill you. You may live in peace now, so please go and tell your wife and your children not to be afraid of me. As a Christian, I do not believe in killing.'

I was not really sure that he understood my words, but he said, 'Thank you so much.' I could tell that he felt relieved to hear these words from me, and I could see that in his smile. Reconciliation can only take place when forgiveness is granted.

As I had promised to tell him more about Jesus Christ, I opened my Bible to read this passage for him:

> For God so loved the world that he gave his one and only Son, that whoever believes in him shall not perish but have eternal life. For God did not send his Son into the world to condemn the world, but to save the world through him. Whoever believes in him is not condemned, but whoever does not believe stands condemned already because he has not believed in the name of God's one and only Son. (John 3:16–18)

After hearing this message, he couldn't fully understand its meaning. It was the first time in his life that he had heard about the Son of God. I took some time to explain this passage to him:

'If you open your heart to receive Jesus Christ as your Lord and Saviour, your sin of killing my family will be forgiven. Let me ask you, if your hands are dirty, what do you use to clean them?'

He said, 'I use soap and water to wash my hands.'

'That's right,' I responded. 'If you believe in Jesus Christ, your sins are forgiven by his blood. Nothing else can wash away your countless sins, except the blood of Jesus Christ.'

He just nodded his head, but I could tell that he didn't really understand what I was trying to say to him. All I heard from him was that he would like to learn more about Jesus Christ, so I promised to come at a later date to tell him more about Christ. Handing him a Bible, I asked him to read the Gospel of John first. I was so glad that he could read. I hugged him and smiled.

Facing the family's killers and saying 'I forgive you' was very painful, because I had embraced anger, bitterness, hatred and the will to take revenge for so long in my life. These emotions had become my precious possessions. Now that God had washed out my negative emotions, I needed to start a new life by cancelling all of these feelings and replacing them with good ones. I know that true forgiveness has to come from a heart willing to accept such a 'second hurt'. My former 'precious possessions' – the destructive emotions – were removed by the Holy Spirit. When saying 'I forgive you', I had felt as though part of my heart was being cut from me, and I believe it was the Holy Spirit's work. Such a cut was painful, but it released me from the bondage of anger, bitterness, hatred and the will to pursue my family's honour. The Holy Spirit replaced anger with a spirit of stillness, bitterness with the joy of life, hatred with love, and the will to pursue honour with the will to forgive. I was in tears, but the tears washed away the pain made by the cut. True forgiveness is a willingness to endure the second hurt, but it brings about healing. 'Nevertheless, I will bring health and healing to it; I will heal my people and will let them enjoy abundant peace and security' (Jeremiah 33:6).

After writing my first book and making the promotional trip abroad, I began to become aware that forgiveness is a very personal discovery. For me it was about finding a way to improve my physical and mental health, my self-esteem and my spiritual journey. This personal discovery has led me down a painful road but, beyond the pain, it has helped me to see the beauty of life. It has also helped me to look at my scars and to know I am healed. I have found inner peace and I no longer live with bitterness. There is the beauty of the rainbow after the heavy rain.

In the past I thought I was totally healed, but it was not true; my painful memories were only manageable. No doubt, I had forgiven my family's murderers, but there was still an old wound that had not been healed in a healthy way. True healing took place only when I went to meet the killers and was reconciled with them. I remember the agony I felt after saying, 'I forgive you' to the man who had killed my father. I felt as though my heart had been cut open, but I now believe this was surgery from the Holy Spirit. After I had forgiven, the scars of anger, bitterness, sadness and resentment had remained, but now I sensed that this was the point when the Holy Spirit removed the scars and replaced them with joy. I couldn't imagine the power of such forgiveness; it felt as though the cancer of my soul had vanished.

Many years earlier, before I was able to forgive, I seemed to flounder in a sea of depression. I experienced headaches, muscle tension, fatigue, sleeping problems and anxiety disorders. I believe that all of these problems resulted from my unwillingness to forgive. I had allowed these problems to fester inside in a way that built up barriers to a wholesome life. My personal desire to take revenge for my family has been melted away by the grace of God. He has softened my heart by taking away the evil desire and putting in its place a heart of compassion. Now he has a special purpose for me – to deliver the message of forgiveness to a broken people.

Forgiveness takes time, and the problems associated with an unforgiving spirit are solved over a period of time. This has been the process by which I am beginning to feel healthy again. I feel an inner liberation; the hatred and bitterness no longer control my life. Rather, I am free from those negative emotions and the big ball of fire that consumed my heart for years has been extinguished. The cancer of my soul is now cured by the healing power of forgiveness. To have lived for so many years with unforgiveness was hellish. There was a time when I thought it was an impossibility to forgive my family's murderers; now I smile to myself that I have been able to forgive and then move on with a beautiful freedom in Christ.

Humanly speaking, complete forgiveness is impossible in these circumstances without the work of the Holy Spirit and the grace of God. Yet I am happy because I feel that I have accomplished my quest for forgiveness, and I thank God for granting me the courage and wisdom to forgive. It was God's abundant grace that inspired and enabled me to forgive the killers for the crimes they had perpetrated against my family.

I would like to conclude this chapter with an email from someone who read *The Tears of My Soul*. Forgiveness from within the human heart is not easy, but it is possible by the grace of God:

Dear Reaksa

I recently read your story *The Tears of My Soul.* I want to thank you for the unusual honesty with which the story is written. Such honesty – painful and brutal – is rare, very rare. I was quite affected. Twenty-six years ago, I suffered a tremendous, unforeseeable, and sudden loss. From this tragedy emerged a person much like your own story: bitter, bewildered, and inconsolable. People, especially Christians, seemed to offer the most hurtful advice; they only made my pain worse. But, over the many years, I have learned to live with the pain but it still has been difficult to accept what happened.

That is why I write to thank you, today. I was moved to read a journey that seemed to parallel my own journey into grief. Your honesty and exposition of your inner feelings appears to have given me a strong sense of belonging. You have made me feel less alone. I, basically, had become unable to express my inner feelings due to the harm that came from the half-dozen times I had done so. Forgiveness seemed to be all but impossible. But, after reading your own journey, I feel there is hope to separate the memories of a terrible tragedy from my ability – or inability – to forgive. I think, now, I can forgive. If you, who suffered so much more, can forgive, then I too will follow your sincerity and forgive, also.

Sincerely

Name supplied

I spoke in more than forty churches in Northern Ireland. Several times I used this letter to close my message about forgiveness. It touched many lives. After I had finished my talk, many people approached me to talk to me about my experience of forgiveness. Some people were struggling with how to forgive: they did not know how to get rid of their bitterness. Others were confused about their forgiveness. Some were asking for a formula so that they could go quickly through the process of forgiveness. There is no such formula. It takes time to go through the emotional storms of personal transformation. I must admit that forgiveness is the most difficult task to accomplish, if you have been badly hurt. I learned that forgiveness is not so much about liberating my enemies, but is rather the art of setting myself free from the bondage of bitterness, hatred and anger. Reconciliation brought me into a higher calling to fulfil my personal duty of healing. Now that God has set me free, I have obeyed his word by forgiving, and I am free from negative emotions. I can see the beauty of life beyond the long, painful journey of forgiveness.

CHAPTER SEVEN

BLESSINGS

'Do not be overcome by evil, but overcome evil with good' (Romans 12:21)

After meeting two of the killers and many other people in the village several times, I realized that these people had never been properly educated. They were still living in a primitive culture and would be trapped in poverty for many generations to come. My heart was filled with compassion for them. This wasn't an easy love for me, but I felt as though the Lord was teaching me to take another step forward to help them. He was asking me to bless them. It took me a year to pray and wait for the funding to come in, but after my trip to promote my book in the United States, Canada, the UK and Singapore, I had enough money to build a school for the village people. So I went back to the village to ask the people to contribute to the building of the school. I spoke to the village chief and asked him to encourage them to be involved in the building project.

I have to admit that what I was doing for these people was not born out of my character or kindness; it was purely the grace of God. Speaking from a human point of view, it is an impossible thing to go back and meet the people who have killed one's family and to bless them. I remembered the day I vowed never to return to Cambodia, the land that had left me with such deep emotional and psychological scars. Now, by the grace of God, I was back to bless them.

These things remind me of the story of Joseph, who was raised in a big family of twelve. His father, Jacob, loved him so much that he became the favourite son in the family, and this created jealousy amongst his eleven brothers which grew into hatred. They plotted to kill him but ultimately decided not to, because he was, after all, their brother. So, instead of killing him, they sold him as a slave. Joseph went through much hardship in his life. He was betrayed and enslaved. He was falsely accused and ended up in prison, where he remained, forsaken and forgotten.

However, after he had completed his course in hardship, the Lord restored him. He was polished and refined by the Lord and became the most powerful man in Egypt, after Pharaoh. Then, when famine became severe in Canaan and starvation seemed inevitable, Jacob sent his ten sons to Egypt to buy grain. Benjamin, the youngest, he kept at home to be a comfort to him. When the ten brothers presented themselves before Joseph, the governor of Egypt, to buy grain, they did not recognize him as their brother. He stood before them now as the mightiest figure in the land. He recognized his brothers at once. They were the ones who had sold him as a slave. Now, they came to buy grain from him.

I believe that Joseph's heart was broken when he saw his brothers again. The biblical account tells us that when Joseph first saw his brothers, he wept (Genesis 42:24). He also wept later when he saw Benjamin (Genesis 43:30). Despite the hardship and pain that his brothers had inflicted on his heart, Joseph bore no grudge against them. I believe that he did not nurture bitterness, hatred, anger or ill feeling against them; rather, he gave them forgiveness. He also treated them kindly and graciously. Humanly speaking, such a thing is impossible, but Joseph forgave his brothers and extended his kindness and generosity to them. His forgiveness did not stop at merely forgiving the brothers who had hurt him so deeply, but extended to a shower of blessing with grain.

There is no question that Joseph absolutely forgave his brothers. He could afford to forget the pain and the events of the past that had been inflicted upon his heart and soul. He wanted to start all over again. He chose forgiveness by letting the affliction go from his heart, and he chose the healing of his wounds. But the pitfall in this story is the brothers' unwillingness to receive Joseph's forgiveness. They were filled with fear and insecurity:

> When Joseph's brothers saw that their father was dead, they said, 'What if Joseph holds a grudge against us and pays us back for all the wrongs we did to him?' So they sent word to Joseph, saying, 'Your father left these instructions before he died: "This is what you are to say to Joseph: I ask you to forgive your brothers the sins and the wrongs they committed in treating you so badly." Now please forgive the sins of the servants of the God of your father.' When their message came to him, Joseph wept. (Genesis 50:15–17)

Joseph's brothers chose to live in the bondage of fear and insecurity. They would live their lives in the trap of fear forever. When I first went to see the man who had killed my father, he displayed no remorse or regret for what he had done to my family. He did not understand the meaning of forgiveness. I remembered how, when I gave him a hug and told him that I forgave him, his body trembled uncontrollably. He was very frightened. I, too, had felt like that when he had led me to the grave. I could remember how terrified I had been before the moment of execution. Now, I could understand the terror he was experiencing when I hugged him. But I told him again and again, trying to reassure him, that I had come to bring peace, not death. I had come to forgive him and be reconciled with him. I had come to cancel the old debt, but he didn't receive the message of forgiveness from me. He was terrified, even though I assured him of my message of forgiveness. Later he told me that after I had left the village, he was unable to sleep for at least a month. Guilt was breeding such insecurity and fear in his life that he was terrified that I would send someone to kill him. He could not imagine that I had come to bring peace and reconciliation. The worst part was that I had taken some of his photos with me. He thought that I would use these to find him in order to kill him. He was afraid of encountering strangers from other villages.

I went to the village several times to share the good news with the people and to talk about the building project, trying to get them involved. They were all so happy, but when I tried to get them to make some contribution to the school, they were reluctant to do so. It took many visits before they got involved. I agreed to provide all the materials and the project supervisors, and the village people were to help by labouring – with the condition that they would receive no payment. They were also to provide food for the supervisors until the school was finished. I sent Pastor Vansan to oversee the whole building project.

Before the project could begin, we had difficulty in bringing materials to the village. No one wanted to transport them because it is such a remote area with no proper road. I spoke to three construction companies, asking them if they would bring materials to the village, but they were reluctant to go. After a while they agreed, but at triple the normal price of all materials. We decided to leave it to the Lord and prayed. Thankfully, one company agreed to go, but they still asked for extra payment. Finally, I agreed to the deal, but on the delivery day, I heard that the lorry bringing the materials had broken down. It was damaged so badly that the extra profit they had earned from me was not enough to cover the repairs.

During the time when the school was being built, Pastors Vansan and Sokcheat shared the good news with the people. As a result, about ten people in the village received Jesus Christ as their Lord and Saviour. Some time later, I invited my church-planting partner, Pastor Pak Soon Lau, to go to the village with me to see the school and to hold our first worship service with the believers there. When we arrived in the village, we began the service at Mr Mead's house. He was a new believer and had formerly been a Buddhist priest. When he stood up to share his new-found faith with us, I was very impressed by his speech; he spoke so intelligently. I could see much potential in his leadership, so we laid our hands on him and prayed for him to be the village church's leader.

Then Mao, the man who had killed my family, also joined us in the worship service. As yet, he has not received Christ as his Lord and Saviour, but I felt highly honoured to have him there with us. After we had sung a few songs and had prayed for the new believers, Pastor Vansan handed the service over to Pastor Pak Soon Lau to deliver his message. He began by speaking in the Khmer language, but after his greetings and introduction, because he didn't feel confident about communicating deep theological content in Khmer, he switched to English, asking me to translate into Khmer for him. This took me by surprise, because he had not told me in advance. He began to tell a story from Genesis about Joseph – how he was raised in the family, was favoured by his father, betrayed by his brothers and sold as a slave. He described how Joseph, after his many sufferings, met his brothers again and forgave them. They did not accept his forgiveness. In his application, Pastor Pak Soon Lau used me as an example – God had saved me and brought me back to the village to forgive the very people who had killed my family:

Reaksa's life is similar to Joseph's story. However, Reaksa has taken a step further than Joseph by coming to look for the people who killed his family, by forgiving them and also by blessing them. Imagine if you were able to live in a peaceful country like Canada, where Reaksa has lived for the last ten years. Would you have come back to forgive the people who killed your family? It is an impossibility. But Reaksa has chosen to travel on a road that not many people would like to travel. It is a painful road. What would he gain from the village? If I were Reaksa, I would not have been able to have the courage to travel this road. But Reaksa's life is a living testimony as to how God is working through his life. It is a life of transformation by the grace of God.

Mao was sitting on my right side. He showed no remorse and no willingness to accept my forgiveness. How could I interpret the sermon when such emotions were being stirred up within me? When I looked at him, I began to weep, and my voice gradually changed. Pastor Pak Soon Lau was aware of my shaky voice. He knew that I could not continue to interpret for him, and he stopped preaching. I could see the terror and guilt in Mao, but I knew he did not know how to deal with it. He still suppressed his emotions, which is the common way of life for him and many other Cambodians. I could see many people in the village, especially in the years after the Khmer Rouge regime, struggling to cope with everyday life, and many others had suffered terrifying and traumatic experiences. Most of them found that the only way to go on was to suppress what had happened to them.

It is not that I have refused to forgive him, but he has not accepted my forgiveness. I know he will continue to live in fear for many years to come, despite my assurance of forgiveness in word and deed. Joseph's story helps me to see the beauty of forgiveness. Not only did he forgive his brothers, he also blessed them. I am now trying to apply his story to my life. It is not as easy to practise this teaching as it is to read Joseph's story. God has changed my life and God's grace has transformed me into a new person. I must now live my life in the newness of Christ.

During the course of building the school, I received much criticism from many friends – believers and non-believers alike. It was hard to accept such destructive comments, but I learned to stand firmly on my decision. I knew that God had a special mission for me to accomplish and that I must not allow this vision to die. I was determined to get the project accomplished. A few of my cousins criticized me for not taking care of my family first before I reached out to help others. They said I always reached out to others and sacrificed for them, but paid less attention to my own family and relatives. They challenged me, 'You do not have a house of your own to live in. Why do you have to build a school for the people who were directly involved in killing your family?'

I did not know how to respond to them, and I must admit that their criticism was true; it revealed a weakness in my character. This criticism made me miserable because it was especially true after some men, intent on stealing his motorbike, had murdered my brother-in-law. My cousins blamed me for not taking better care of my relatives. If I had given some money to help my sister's family, my brother-in-law would not have needed to use a motorbike so late in the evening, and he would not have been robbed and killed. I felt guilty and depressed and was overwhelmed by such turmoil amongst my own relatives.

I could not settle down to writing again and was trapped by this destructive criticism. Barely able to escape from this trap, I was deeply hurt and confused. I couldn't eat or sleep properly for several weeks after my brother-in-law was killed. I even lost my interest in reading the Bible for my own daily devotions. Then I tried to read the Bible to find out more on the topic of forgiveness, but I could not really understand what I was reading. I had been hit by storms so many times in my life; now, after I thought the storms had subsided, I was hit by a tornado. The impact of such criticism over-whelmed me. How should I take it?

Some accused me of being a silly man who had been brainwashed by the Western religion of Christianity. If I had not gone to study in the Western world, I would not be doing such ridiculous things. This was, perhaps, very true and I don't deny it. If I were not a Christian, I would not be doing the things they accused me of; I would be taking revenge for my family. These people saw me as an intruder and a troublemaker in their society. I am sure it makes sense to them, because they do not know how to forgive. They do not see the beauty of forgiveness and they do not know how to be set free from the bondage of bitterness, anger and hatred. Looking at the other side of the coin, I believe these people are trapped by their unforgiveness. They will be trapped for life, and even if they wanted to get out, they would not know how. They are not aware of the consequence of unforgiveness, the reality of which is living in darkness and moving to a slow death.

Others blamed me for destroying society. Trying to defend their logic, they said, 'They once killed your fam-ily. Now, you come back to the village and bring medicine and clothes. You dig wells and even build a school for them. Next, they will kill more people so that you come back to build a city for them. They should be tried and punished, not blessed. This should not be allowed. Something must be wrong in your head.'

This criticism is born out of human nature. I know that this makes sense according to their logic, but it does not make sense according to God's. I was speechless when I heard such negative remarks. Examining the sit-uation from their perspective, I am a troublemaker or an intruder, but I know that God is pleased with me. I knew that these people were laughing at me and I knew that the devil would always try to find a way to obstruct my obedience to the Lord. This forgiveness is simply an act of obedience. This blessing is a calling from the Lord to a higher level of forgiveness. God has forgiven my countless sins, so in gratitude, it is right for me to forgive my family's killers. I must not live by what people say about me, but I must rely on biblical teaching, seeking to imitate my Lord's example. If Joseph could do it, I also can do it – and so can you.

The school is a symbol of my forgiveness to the people in the village. It contains only two classrooms but each room can take up to sixty students. I also provided furniture for each classroom. Funds used to build this school were collected in the form of many gifts and from my book sales during my promotional trip overseas. I thank God for bringing me into contact with those generous people. I decided to name the school 'God's Grace Primary School: Kokpreach'. I really love the words 'God's Grace'. It was by God's grace that I could forgive my family's killers, and I am blessing them with this school as a symbol of my forgiveness.

On 1 October 2004, the school was dedicated for the use of the village people. More than 200 came for this special dedication, and my heart was filled with mixed emotions – happiness and sadness. I was happy to see what I had done for the people in this village, even though it was, humanly speaking, impossible. I would never have dreamed of doing such a thing, but the grace of God motivated me to finish this formidable mission. At the same time I felt sad, because none of my relatives and parents were there to see that I had accomplished this seemingly impossible project to help my people. My heart would have been filled with tremendous joy if they had been with me at this dedication ceremony. All I can do is learn to live with no parents or family. If my parents had been there, they would have said, 'Well done, son. We're very proud of you.'

I invited three people (the village chief, a commune representative and my foster-father Mov) from the village to cut the ribbon to start the ceremony. I cut the final ribbon, and the village chief and the commune representative gave their speeches of appreciation. I felt honoured to speak to the people from the villages:

> Good morning. It is a special privilege for me to be with you this morning. It is good to be back to see many old friends, and others whom I do not recognize at all. First of all, I want to thank God for sparing my life. God has a special purpose for me to bring you a message of forgiveness today. Before I address you, let me assure you again that it is God's grace that brings me back here today, and I thank God so much for this special day.
>
> I have heard that many people in the village have been speculating that I was building this school in order to pay gratitude and respect to my family. Others have been speculating that I am trying to build up merit points in this life so that I will be intelligent in the next one. Now, I'd like you to allow me to explain that none of these speculations is correct. I have built this school for two reasons. Firstly, this school is a symbol of my forgiveness of the people in this village, and I believe you are aware of what happened to my family more than twenty years ago. They were killed here but I survived the execution, and I thank God for sparing my life. Do you know how I felt after my family was killed? I lived with painful memories that can never be forgotten.

I have experienced trauma, nightmares and depression. When I was in the grave, I had no hope that I would have a day like this. But God took me from the grave and restored my life. He has taken me on a long, painful journey back here to deal with this unwanted emotional legacy. It took me many years to learn to forgive and it was very hard. I never thought that I could return to this village with a blessing for you, but God has a special mission for me.

Do you know the reason I decided to name this school 'God's Grace Primary School'? This is to serve as a reminder that I am alive today because of God's grace in my life. It is not my own fortune [or *bonn*, meaning merited credit] that saved me. Rather, it is absolutely God's grace. The moment I was hit from behind and fell into the grave with many other victims is beyond many people's imagination. If God had not saved me that day, someone might have buried me; I might not have had the chance to speak to you today. God's grace is so amazing. What God has done in my life is truly a work of his amazing grace. Only that grace could enable me to forgive you and bless you with this school. This blessing is born out of God's grace, not my generous heart. You know this act of forgiveness and blessing would be impossible on a human level, but it is possible with God.

It is not easy to learn to forgive. For some of you, if someone steals something from you, just a small thing, what you often do is pick up your axe in order to chase and kill the thief. This is a common practice here in this village. You are not able to forgive just a small thing. But my whole family was butchered in front of me. How do you think I feel? Yet, despite the hurt, bitterness and anger, I have learned to forgive. Frankly, years ago, I longed to take revenge for my family. I could not forget the first promise I had made in front of my family's grave. Some of you were aware that I was a policeman in the city. A few of you have mentioned to me that you did not have the courage to go to the city, because you were afraid of me. I will be very honest with you. If I had seen you while I was a policeman, I would have killed you all. At that time, I was deeply influenced by the pursuit of family honour – revenge was my top priority. But many years after I had become a Christian, God helped me to learn to forgive. First, he forgave my countless sins, and then he helped me to liberate myself from the bondage of bitterness. It is morally right for me to forgive you. Forgiveness was given as a gift from God for me. Now, I would like to pass on this gift of God to you. This school is my symbol of forgiveness for you. It is a blessing from a Christian brother and part of the history of forgiveness in this village. I believe that none of you can do this yet, but if you are angry with someone, or if someone wrongs you or hurts you in any way, please remember my example of forgiveness. Please do not kill any more innocent people. Please learn to live with each other in peace and harmony.

Secondly, I built this school for you and for your children. I would like your children to move out of the bondage of poverty and have a better life. I would like them to learn how to read. I strongly believe that education brings a better understanding in life. My late father used to teach me, 'A man without knowledge will always be brought down by what he does not understand.' It will help your children to move out of this primitive culture. I want to see your children living not with blood on their hands, but in peaceful harmony with each other.

What I would like to see in the future is that some of the children who come to study in this school, ten to fifteen years from now, will come back to teach here. I would like to see a bright future for your children in the next generation. Please do not forget to remind your children that this school is a symbol of forgiveness from a Christian brother who lost his family in this village, and who chose to forgive instead of taking revenge. Jesus said, 'Love your enemies, do good to those who hate you, bless those who curse you, pray for those who mistreat you' (Luke 6:27–28). This is the most important teaching in Christian life. This school is the symbol of my forgiveness and, through it, I demonstrate my love to you. It is the grace of God that has transformed my hatred into love. I never thought I could accomplish this difficult task. I am just a simple human being like you; I feel weak. I must sincerely confess to you that I do not have the emotional energy to turn hatred into love, but God has given me the strength to achieve this. I know that nothing is impossible with God.

Before I end my speech this morning, may I ask you to take care of this school? I am not asking you to do it for me, but for yourselves; it is not my school, but yours. Please keep it well maintained. A Christian sister who has contributed funds to help this school sends her word of encouragement to you. She gives her greetings and hearty congratulations to you. Her prayer for you is that you will be much blessed by the teaching that you will receive at the school and that you will be able to understand and experience God's love for you. She gives her wish that you will cherish and protect the school and do your best to make sure that only good things are taught here and that it will be used only for good things. Every time you see the school, may you remember that Jesus loves you very much. Once again, thank you so much for giving me an opportunity to speak to you this morning. May this school be a blessing to your children. May God richly bless you.

After finishing my speech, I distributed hundreds of notebooks and pens to children and teachers in the village. About 200 children would attend the school. I also gave notebooks and pens to two new teachers who had been sent by the government to teach the children. I took a moment to speak to them and encouraged them to teach good things to the children of this village.

I also spoke to Mao, the man who had killed my father. He was so happy to see the school that he had brought his five children to the dedication and told me that three of his children would come to study there. I blessed him and his children and also assured him of my forgiveness: 'This is my symbol of forgiveness for you. Whenever you pass by this school, you know that I have forgiven you.' He did not know what to say to me but he gave me a big smile. That, at least, was a sign of acceptance. My prayer for him is that he will surrender himself to the Lord and let him provide liberation from the bondage of guilt. Ean, the one who had killed my mother, could not come for the dedication because he was not at home. I wished he could have heard me speaking the message of forgiveness. However, I am sure that he will be happy to see the school and that he too will send his younger children to it.

What I have done for the people in this village is to demonstrate my love to them. This school is not only the symbol of my forgiveness, it is also the legacy of my love for the village people. Now, I feel liberated from the pain of my past; forgiveness gives me the freedom to move on. This practice of love for my enemies reflects the teaching of Jesus Christ in my life. I forgive them, not only to demonstrate my love for them, but also to show that I am a new person, a dearly loved child of God. Since Christ loves me, I can pass on that love to my enemies. I do pray that they open their hearts to accept the love of Jesus Christ.

I do not think that these people really understand what I have said about forgiveness, because there is no such teaching in their society; in their minds, forgiving means forgetting. What I have done for them would be interpreted as releasing my debt. They think I must have owed them something in my previous life, so in this life I have returned to pay them back. Their minds are trapped by the doctrine of *karma* and they think that I have come back to release my *karma*. Even though they do not understand what I have done for them, it is confirmed by the blessings that I have as a result of my obedience to God. The heavy rain has fallen in my life, quenching forever the fire of resentment, which gave me so much pain. Now the sky is clear again.

Before I returned home, I walked round the school and thanked the Lord for sparing my life. He has transformed me, turning my evil intent into blessing. He brought me back to bless the people who had hurt me the most, and I know he has a special mission for me in bringing this message of forgiveness to my people. It has been hard, but I thank God for taking me along the journey of pain and suffering onto a higher level of forgiving and blessing my former enemies.

A few months after the school dedication, I went back to the village to visit Pastor Mead and to encourage him to be faithful to the Lord. I also went to see the school. It was exhilarating to see it filled with students. I believe they will remember me, but my greatest longing is to see them all coming to knowledge of Christ Jesus as Saviour and Lord.

If my parents were alive to see what I have done, they would be proud of me. But they are gone forever. I know the Lord is walking with me and I am part of the family of God. What a wonderful fact it is that I am God's son and he is my Father, when I have no earthly father. He seems to say, 'Good job, my son. I am proud of you. You have imitated my example.' My heart is filled with joy. Painful memories and emotional stresses have been banished from my heart, and it is all by *the grace of God*.

I regularly visit Pastor Mead to train him into a leadership role in the small church. I thank God for him because he is faithful to the Lord, despite his lack of knowledge. His church is beginning to grow and he has a passion for the Lord and wants to plant churches. I encourage him to go slowly and, most importantly, he needs time to grow in his walk with God.

A year after the school had been built, the village was hit by a famine. I remembered how many years ago, I experienced starvation in this very village. I had to force myself to eat many different kinds of edible leaves; I ate bamboo shoots for almost three months. So I helped Pastor Mead to ship five tons of rice for distribution to the starving people. In addition, I arranged for some medical missionaries from South Korea and the United States to do check-ups for the village people. It was the first time in their lives that they had been treated by foreign medical doctors.

The distance to the village from Siemreap city is about ninety kilometres. We left the city by bus at 7 a.m. and arrived at 11.30 a.m. About half-way to the village, we transferred into five tractor-pulled carts because of the poor state of the roads. When we arrived, Pastor Mead arranged to have a few hundred people from the village waiting for us at the school. Although we were a little late, the people gathered in a circle and said a short prayer. One member from the medical team gave a short gospel message:

Greetings. We arrived a bit late, but we thank the Lord for bringing us here to bless you. We are Christians from Bayside Church, California. It is a special privilege for us to work along with Reaksa. He has told us a lot about this place, especially about God's Grace Primary School, a symbol of his forgiveness. We are so excited to be here. We would like to bless you with the service this morning. Once again, thank you so much and we thank Pastor Mead who has arranged for you to come for medical treatment. We might not be able to see all the people, but we will do our best. May God bless you.

After the short message, we had the people quickly line up to see the doctors and dentists. We worked hard until 3 p.m. without stopping for lunch, but we still did not see all of them. We had to rush back home, because the journey is very difficult and we needed to be back before dark. We were concerned that if the bus broke down on the road before we reached the city, we would face a dangerous situation. The leader of the medical team wrote to me after he had returned to the USA:

Dear Reaksa,
Greetings from California in the name of our Lord and Saviour Jesus Christ!
I would like to thank you for hosting our medical team to visit the village where you lost your family. I have learned a lot from you during my trip to Cambodia, especially, the notion of forgiveness, central to Christ's message, remains illusory for so many of us. I have shared your story with countless friends, Christians and non-Christians alike. Even among serious believers, the level of forgiveness God has allowed you to demonstrate is far beyond what any of us have experienced or truly empathized. When I first heard your story I was impressed, overwhelmed.

Intellectually it was understandable. Dwelling on the reality of the entire process, though, was unfathomable, completely incomprehensible. It made me pray: 'I get it, Lord. I get it. Thank you for Reaksa's example. Please don't ever test me like that.' My visceral, gut response to evil as a man, as a husband and father, as a former Marine, is to want to personally kill, seek retribution, destroy, and wipe out completely. Having met and worked with you on one mission trip and your subsequent visit to America, having read and re-read your book, I had grown a bit more used to what was exceptional. When you asked our medical team to go out and work in the very place where your family was murdered, where two of the soldiers personally responsible for their execution lived, where you had gone back to specifically forgive these men, where God had led you to build a school so that his truth might be proclaimed, we were intrigued, to say the least. Each of us inwardly asked: 'Could I do this?' The universal answer was a resounding: 'No!' None of us alone could forgive that level of evil. But neither, probably, could you alone, but as you had mentioned to us, 'God's grace is your life.' If one needs further proof that God exists – all they need do is observe your faithful witness.

Talking about going to your village and actually going there were two different things. Except for being quite remote – it took us almost five hours over tortuous roads each way to get there – the village in many ways was not unlike the dozens of others we have worked in over the years. It was one thing to read about a man whom you forgave. It was quite another to stand next to him, look him in the eye, imagine what possessed him those not too many years ago to do what he did, to live so completely in the abyss with no hope at all, and now see that God is at work in your life, Reaksa. Knowing what has gone on, what is going on now, and what is likely to come from God's special blessings is an example few people are able to personally observe. Individually and collectively our group could only marvel at what God has begun there in the middle of rural Cambodia, a million miles from our own realities. As we left the village that day, it was not quite clear to me as to who had been ministered to and blessed more, those in the village or those on our medical team. We were all lifted up and continue to be lifted up by the work God is doing through you at God's Grace Primary School, Kokpreach. We would still all pray, 'Please, God, don't test me like that.' Reaksa, your life is more like Joseph. Once again, thank you for hosting our medical team. I will keep praying for your ministry.

Your brother in the Lord
Richard Botkin

As I reflect about this, I cannot hold back my tears. They are not tears of sadness, but tears of joy. I thank the Lord for sparing my life. Jesus said, 'I have come into the world as a light, so that no one who believes in me should stay in darkness' (John 12:46). The country of Cambodia has been through a period of great darkness and the only hope for this land is the message of forgiveness. This teaching is unknown in our culture, and there are many former Khmer Rouge soldiers, who killed thousands of innocent people, still living in freedom. Some are being brought to trial, but whether there can be fair trials in a country that has a large degree of corruption, no one knows. Up to the time of writing, the Cambodian government and the UN war-crime tribunal have been trying so hard to put the remaining Khmer Rouge leaders on trial. Many Cambodians who lost their relatives during the darkest period are very suspicious about the trial and believe that those arranging the process are only attempting to play 'good guy and bad guy'. The majority of Cambodians believe that trying just a few remaining Khmer Rouge leaders will never achieve real justice for the victims of the Killing Fields. Cambodians would like to see those outside Cambodia, (especially foreign governments) who were behind the Khmer Rouge regime, put on trial too. Generally speaking, human courts do not always deliver justice, but our God is a God of justice, and it is his role to avenge evil, never ours.

My role is to bless my people in the area surrounding Siemreap, and God has blessed the work. I have had to come to terms with the criticisms and realize that although I am doing God's will, this will not always please the people, and they may not always appreciate what has been done to help them move forward. However, as I look at this area, so full of memories of my painful past, I now see the miracle that God has performed in the five areas where there are growing churches praising his great name every week. We are seeing new converts too, and the general welfare of the people has been helped by visiting missionaries. There has been a thriving women's fellowship planted by a lady doctor from OMF. Pastor Mead invites her to speak to the faithful women who meet together monthly in Kokpreach village.

All five house churches met together for the Khmer New Year celebrations, and it was a special blessing to hear their praises ringing out in the countryside that years ago was a Killing Field. All this is a wonderful tribute to a faithful God who rescued me from the grave, brought me to know his wonderful salvation in Jesus Christ, taught me to obey his teachings of forgiveness, and blessed my life in a way I never dreamed would be possible. My wife Phaly is a support to me, and my lovely children Philos and Sophia bring me such joy.

There are now five small churches in the very countryside where my family lie buried, and my vision is to plant more. There are clean water wells for the people to drink and a school to educate the next generation. It is my hope and prayer that they will come to know the Light of the World who is the only one who can dispel the darkness brought about by the evil one. God has given me a role similar to that of Joseph, who forgave his brothers and became a blessing to them. In the process of learning to forgive and putting that great Christian teaching into practice in a way that was extremely painful to me, the heavy rain has cleared and the tears of my soul have been wiped away. I can see the beauty of the rainbow after the heavy rain in my life.

CONTACT THE AUTHOR

If you would like to contact Sokreaksa S. Himm, please email him at this address: tohimm@yahoo.ca

SAO Cambodia originated in 1973, through the witness of a Cambodian Christian – Chhirc Taing – who was studying in the UK. He returned to Cambodia at the request of the Cambodian Church, where, in 1975, he lost his life as the Khmer Rouge took hold of the country.

For over 30 years, we have sought to be faithful to his calling by raising awareness and helping with refugees outside Cambodia and, since 1990, through our involvement in the country, promoting the Christian faith and seeking to relieve poverty and distress amongst its people.

To find out more about the work of SAO Cambodia please visit our website: www.saocambodia.org